"Our numbers around health are alarming, We even have a special diabetes that they call the Flatbush diabetes. People do not realize their behaviors are causing their illnesses. We need to stop treating symptoms and start treating the underlying problems."

— *Eric Adams, Brooklyn Borough President*
NY Times Article 3.23.17

"A deeply sourced, brilliant prescription for what healthcare must be in the 21st century."

— *Robert Hayes President & CEO*
Community Health Network

"David Woodlock in his insightful book, entitled Emotional Dimensions of Healthcare, lays out a compelling array of facts that aim at getting at the heart of our current healthcare system and its regrettably poor outcomes. The book takes you through the medical and social science of health and illnesses and posits that much of what we are currently doing is not working and we need to conceptualize differently the approach to health and wellbeing. David offers up some examples of behavioral and social intervention that if applied holistically would be able to move the needle on improving our country's healthcare outcomes and the lives of many Americans. This is a thought-provoking book that makes you think differently about how we are approaching these chronic conditions and what we need to do to make an impact. These changes need to happen on the personal, medical and social policy; local and ultimately national level if we want, as David states in this book, a "prescription for better health." "

— Jorge R. Petit, MD
Beacon Health Options

"Simple Truths emerge from complexity; that's what this book has done. Chronic diseases have confounded us for decades, now Woodlock offers an insightful and profoundly meaningful pathway to better health, lower costs and as importantly a deeper personal connection between physican and patient. It also provides an entirely new opportunity for the behavioral health community to become a meaningful and lasting player in an ever-changing healthcare landscape."

— Linda Rosenberg, President & CEO
National Council For Behavioral Health

EMOTIONAL
DIMENSIONS OF
HEALTHCARE

Book design by:
Arbor Services, Inc.
www.arborservices.co/

Printed in the United States of America

Emotional Dimensions of Healthcare
David Woodlock

1. Title 2. Author 3. Healthcare

Library of Congress Control Number: 2017935670
ISBN 13: 978-0-69-285538-6

EMOTIONAL
DIMENSIONS OF
HEALTHCARE

DAVID WOODLOCK

*This book is dedicated to my wonderful wife Kristin
and to my children Dave, Kate , Maggie and Emma*

Contents

Contents

Introduction

When we consider the entire span of thousands of years of human history, remarkably, only a short time ago, physicians—or healers—had little power to cure disease.

To be sure, ancient doctors possessed some real skills in other areas, such as performing amputations and setting broken bones. And there are records of trepanning—a surgical intervention in which a hole is drilled or scraped into the human skull—being successfully performed from Neolithic times onward.

But despite these successes in the external manipulation of the body, for millennia the *inner workings* of the living body remained a mystery. People got sick and died, and no one knew why. Was illness caused by evil spirits, a lack of moral values, or perhaps an imbalance of the four humors—blood, yellow bile, black bile, and phlegm? No one knew for sure. Sometimes the scourge of disease was truly frightful, as in the years 1346 to 1353 when the Black Death killed half of the population of Europe. No one knew what caused it, how to treat it, or how to prevent it. Theories about the source of the Black Death were abundant, ranging from a punishment from God to planetary alignment to evil stares. Many people believed that the plague signaled the Apocalypse, or the end of time. Simon de Covino, the Belgian astronomer who first coined the term "black death" (*mors nigra*), attributed the plague to a conjunction of the planets Jupiter and

Saturn. We now believe it was caused by *Yersinia pestis bacterium*, a form of plague spread by the rat flea; but in spite of the best available science and all the available training, this information was unknown to medieval doctors.

In 1676, using a microscope, an amateur Dutch scientist named Antony van Leeuwenhoek was the first person to see and describe single-cell organisms, which he called "animalcules." This supported the emerging germ theory of disease, first proposed by Girolamo Fracastoro in 1546 and expanded upon by Marcus von Plenciz in 1762, which states that many diseases are caused by microorganisms growing and reproducing within their hosts. Despite mounting evidence, for centuries academics rejected the germ theory in favor of Galen's miasma theory, which held that diseases such as cholera, chlamydia, and the Black Death were caused by a miasma (Greek for "pollution"), a noxious form of "bad air," also known as "night air."

Another breakthrough came in 1854, when a London physician named John Snow scientifically investigated the pattern of an outbreak of cholera. Snow created a map to illustrate how cases of cholera were clustered around a public water pump located in Soho. Why this particular pump? They didn't know it at the time—the action of bacterial infection was still undiscovered—but the cause of the disease was bacteria from human fecal matter. For years, the medical establishment resisted Snow's conclusion, but eventually he was proven right.

In each of these instances and in thousands more like them, the evidence for new ways of thinking was right in front of healers. They used current standards of practice to do what they thought was the right thing on behalf of their patients.

Over the centuries, despite disagreements and resistance, by fits and starts Western medicine continued to make real progress. Physicians began to appreciate the power of the mind to influence the health of the body, and in his controversial 1895 book *Studies in Hysteria*, Sigmund Freud proposed that previously inexplicable physical symptoms were often the surface manifestations of deeply repressed emotional conflicts.

By the early twentieth century doctors had acquired a basic understanding of how the human body gets sick. Throughout the century we saw amazing advances in the knowledge of the intricacies of the human body, and eventually we could even map our DNA. In industrial nations, lifespans continued to get longer, and fewer people died from preventable diseases. And during the twenty-first century we've seen remarkable advances in our ability to repair physical injuries to accident victims and battlefield soldiers, so that injuries that were once fatal are now often survivable.

But something is happening, and it's not good. In the United States, the wealthiest nation in human history, despite our incredible advances in medical technology and the massive amounts of money we spend on our health care, we've hit a wall.

In 2015, the average life expectancy of Americans declined. The many causes included rising numbers of deaths from diabetes, heart disease and stroke, accidents, drug overdoses, and other causes. The most common conditions were heart disease and cancer, accounting for nearly half of all deaths. Deaths from unintentional injuries, which include overdoses from alcohol, drugs, and other substances, as well as motor vehicle crashes and other accidents, have risen. In recent years, public health authorities have dealt with an epidemic of overdoses from prescription narcotics and heroin. Deaths from suicide, the tenth-leading cause of death in the United States, have risen.

Many of these causes of death are notably "lifestyle" diseases that are considered preventable. By way of explanation, some diseases are unavoidable. For example, the influenza pandemic of 1918–1919 killed fifty million people worldwide. The disease killed indiscriminately but was most deadly for people ages twenty to forty, including tens of thousands of frontline soldiers fighting in Europe. It killed so quickly that victims both poor and wealthy literally dropped dead in the streets. At the time, victims could do nothing to escape their fate.

What we are seeing today is something quite different, in which a significant amount of disease can be traced directly to human behavior.

Similar rises in mortality are not being seen in most other Western industrialized nations, which means we need to determine what is unique about health, health care, and socioeconomic conditions in the United States. According to research, Americans are sicker than people in other wealthy industrialized countries, and in some states of the Union, progress on curbing the tide of basic diseases like diabetes is too slow, having stalled or even reversed itself.

How can this be happening? Our knowledge of the inner workings of the human body is extraordinary. We know the mechanistic causes of disease—how viruses attack us, how a stroke happens, how obesity affects the body. We have drugs for nearly every conceivable condition; in fact, the average adult American takes a dozen prescription drugs every year. We have machines that allow us to see inside every nook and cranny of the living body. We have sophisticated tests that can detect the presence of disease long before it reveals itself with symptoms.

Clearly, technology and money are not the only answers to preventing disease and promoting good health. There must be something else, and it's not simply providing better access to the existing system or making medical care cheaper—although both goals are good ones. What's becoming clear is that throughout history we've taken leaps in improving human health, and now it's time for us to take the next great step forward. It begins with recognizing that our bodies are not just machines controlled by our intellect. If that were the case, it would be easy to cure or prevent most chronic disease. All you'd have to do is say, "I know that if I adopt a certain healthy behavior, my health will improve." As we'll see in this book, one of the things that drives doctors crazy is the seeming unwillingness of their patients to do the obvious things that will improve their health. When your doctor says, "If you don't stop eating sweets and gaining weight, you'll get diabetes and shorten your life," what rational person wouldn't immediately change their diet?

The paradox is that in the face of chronic disease and even potential death, plenty of rational people *choose* to continue to eat carbohydrates and sweets. They *choose* to continue to smoke or drink too much. They *choose* to remain sedentary or in isolation all day rather than getting out and exercising. What is driving this? There is a *why* at play here, driven by the pervasiveness of stress, anxiety, adverse childhood experiences, social determinants of health, and unique characteristics in American culture.

These seemingly irrational choices relieve emotional stress and bring real, if temporary, comfort.

Without an understanding of the "why," it's easy to blame the patient. We should *not* be saying, "It's your fault you lack motivation or you are health illiterate." We don't blame the child who gets the measles, and we shouldn't blame the adult who has an eating disorder because they were molested as a child. The point is that human beings are exquisitely complex organisms.

This book is about taking the next leap forward, from the mechanistic view of medicine—which, I'll freely acknowledge, is pretty amazing when you see conjoined twins surgically separated—to a view of health care that embraces not only the visible disease but the emotional dimension that is equally important to good health. Good health depends not only on intellect and body, but on the emotions as well. In this book we'll see how, over and over again, adverse childhood events (ACEs) have been shown to have powerful emotional effects that can influence one's health for a lifetime. These negative effects are often not simply because the person has an unpleasant memory of the event, but because a sufficiently powerful ACE, or a string of them, can *measurably* and *permanently* alter the chemistry of the body itself.

What does this mean?

Imagine that you're walking in the woods on a peaceful day. The sun is shining and the birds are chirping. You feel relaxed. Suddenly a bear looms up in front of you. With a snarl, it starts to chase you. Terrified, you turn and run as fast as you can. Your heart pounds and you shake with fear. Being pursued by a bear is quite an adverse experience!

Then the bear stops chasing you. You look behind you and the bear is gone. You know you can safely stop running. As you cool off, you rely upon your ability to attain homeostasis, which is the tendency of the body to find and stay at a condition of equilibrium or balance within its internal environment. This means that now that the threat has been removed, you can stop running and resume your normal speed of walking at a leisurely pace.

Instead, something strange has happened. Your legs won't slow down. Your body won't stop shaking. You keep running. You know you *can* stop and you *should* stop, but what you want doesn't matter; your legs keep pumping. It's like a switch has been thrown inside you, putting your body into permanent overdrive.

The adverse event has caused a permanent change within you. You now have a "new normal," which is to run at top speed. You can never slow down. For weeks, months, even years you keep running.

If you get sick, or if you engage in unhealthy behavior, your treatment needs to be put into the context of your new normal. And as the years go by, your health history may look quite different from someone who has experienced only enjoyable and relaxing walks in the woods and has never been chased by a bear.

This book explores how chronic stress, adverse childhood experiences, and continued negative social determinants such as exposure to community violence and poverty, can create a new normal in anyone, and how our current approach to health care, with all of its amazing technological advances, isn't coping with the emotional component of health. It's not a trivial issue; as we'll see, the cost of this failure to our nation and its citizens is high and getting higher.

There is hope. In this book I'll survey many of the attempts that have been made to take a holistic approach to health care in which the patient's emotional history is paramount. Some of these efforts have been more fruitful than others. I'll also provide a prescription for better health, featuring innovative ideas already being tried as well as the best ideas that are as yet untried. The result is a roadmap to a new era of health care that can bring a renewal of both longevity and quality of life for millions of Americans.

Chapter 1:

Something's Wrong with America's Health Care System

Roy is a fifty-five-year-old married man who had a heart attack a few months ago. After undergoing a battery of diagnostic tests, he was told by his cardiologist that he's stable now. But while he appears to be healthy, he's convinced that exertion could trigger another heart attack, and his personal life is miserable. He has stopped being intimate with his wife, and instead of going upstairs to bed at night he sleeps on the living room sofa. The last few times he has tried to cut the grass with the lawn mower, he's called an ambulance because he's concerned about how he feels. His doctor tells him repeatedly there's nothing wrong with his heart and suggests he sees a colleague who is a psychiatrist. Roy cannot understand why his doctor would come to such a conclusion; the symptoms he feels are physical, not mental, and he thinks, "There's no way I'm crazy!" Even if Roy would go to the psychiatrist, his insurance would likely not pay for ongoing therapy due to a failure to meet medical necessity criteria.

Without a significant change, Roy's health will most likely continue to deteriorate and the cost of his care will go up, leading to poor outcomes and poor life quality until, perhaps, he really does have another heart attack.

Janice is a forty-year-old woman with chronically unstable diabetes. She lives in a challenging community where violence and poverty are rampant. Each time she's taken to the hospital, her doctor, thoroughly and with great compassion, explains to her the correlation between her fainting episodes and her overeating of cakes and sweets. Each time Janice replies, "Thanks, doctor—I'll try to do better." This replays itself so often the doctor becomes frustrated because he's seemingly doing all the right things and giving her all the medically right treatment in a compassionate way. In a moment of exasperation, he says to her, "If you don't start listening to me, I'm going to have to cut your feet off!" Janice, thoroughly frightened, never returns to his care and continues to eat all the sweet treats that her doctor has urged her to avoid.

In my own family, on a raining morning many years ago, my eldest daughter was driving her two sisters to the store. They were involved in a horrific car accident that nearly killed one of the youngest. At the bedside of my daughter in the ICU, a psychiatrist visited as part of the treatment team. She spoke with each of us, assessed us for psychiatric disorders—of which she saw none—and said that we should call her if we had additional problems.

Many years later, my eldest daughter, the driver of the car, found herself in a drug and alcohol rehab program, and to this day points to the period immediately after the accident when her substance abuse began.

In the United States today are millions of us like Roy, Janice, my family or friends, neighbors, members of your own family, or perhaps even you. We all have access to what should be the finest health care system in the world, and yet we have persistent health problems that seem to defy treatment.

Our Health Care System Is Well Intentioned—And Failing to Connect the Dots

The American health care system is the world's most technically sophisticated and expensive, and yet one of the most ineffective. We've ignored important forces that shape longevity and well-being as much as medical advances and technology elements that we've taken as a measure of our success. These difficult-to-measure elements include the social determinants of health, health disparities, chronic disease management, serious mental health issues, and adverse childhood experiences. What could these seemingly disparate phenomena have in common? While health care in this country has advanced exponentially in its technical ability to diagnose and treat any number of profoundly complex and confounding diseases, we have failed to connect the dots—the emotional dimensions of health care—that make us human and influence the choices we make every day that all too often lead to illness.

Reflecting on the last fifty years, our science, public policy, and public opinion have focused on things we can measure quickly and efficiently, such as contacts, billable hours, hospitalizations, and deaths. Providers want to do more procedures, while patients want every test they can get, open networks, and all of the latest high-tech instrumentation and pharmaceuticals they have seen advertised on television.

Health technology and patient education opportunities have expanded dramatically. We can engineer a patient's own immune cells to target cancer, we have amazing diagnostic machinery, and we have an instant free health care library in the form of the Internet. In the United States, we all—health care providers and patients alike—perceive dramatic benefits, and yet chronic disease continues to get the better of us. With us humans, at the end of the day, getting healthy or curing disease is not as simple as replacing the oil in the family car. We have science and then we have human behavior. People make choices—overeating, drinking, not exercising—and they make them in the face of overwhelming evidence on the crushing impact of these behaviors on their health. In recent years, many have made efforts to improve the quality and outcomes of our chronic disease management efforts, such as visiting nurse programs, in-home supports for diabetes management, text message reminders. Most, if not all, of these have shown only modest improvements in outcomes. Why? Because we are treating the symptoms and not the root causes. The two strongest markers of our failing to connect the dots that lead to health outcome improvement can be seen in the cost vs. outcome gap in American health care and in our growing consumption of medications to treat symptoms.

Our Expensive Health Care System

In our efforts to help people like Roy, Janice, and my daughter, the problem is not a lack of money.

In 2015 the Commonwealth Fund, a private foundation based in New York City that seeks to promote excellence in our health care system, released its report entitled "US Health Care from a Global Perspective: Spending, Use of Services, Prices, and Health in Thirteen Countries." This report compared metrics including utilization, prices, supply, health care spending, and health outcomes across thirteen high-income countries: the United States, France, Australia, Germany, Canada, Netherlands, Denmark, Norway, Japan, New Zealand, Switzerland, and the United Kingdom. The Commonwealth Fund confirmed two facts that many Americans have long suspected but couldn't verify: Overall, the United States spends more on health care than other high-income countries but has worse outcomes. This spending disparity is linked with excessive spending for some and inadequate spending for others. For example, we see the unnecessary use of high-tech diagnostics and other tests for the well insured in contrast to poor access to primary care in distressed communities. For all of our advances, chronic disease management or the lack thereof is one of the primary culprits in our high health care spending.

In discussions of health care reform, much is being written and spoken about data—big data, data analytics, and data informing precision medicine. Health systems and health policy gurus are virtually overwhelmed with data. As McKinsey & Company wrote,

"Physicians have traditionally used their judgment when making treatment decisions, but in the last few years there has been a move toward evidence-based medicine, which involves systematically reviewing clinical data and making treatment decisions based on the best available information. Aggregating individual data sets into big-data algorithms often provides the most robust evidence, since nuances in subpopulations (such as the presence of patients with gluten allergies) may be so rare that they are not readily apparent in small samples." This may be true, but it overlooks a huge factor in the health of every individual, and there is almost no data on people's emotional well-being, their stress levels, or compensatory needs and behaviors.

In 2016, another report by the Commonwealth Fund revealed that not only are Americans in poorer health, but when they're sick the high cost of care makes them more likely than others to go without recommended health care, avoid the doctor, or fail to fill a prescription.

As reported by Shelby Livingston in *Modern Healthcare*, about a third of US adults said they skipped needed health care because they couldn't afford it. While this figure represents a small improvement over the rate of 37% in the previous 2013 survey, adults in the US consistently say they face greater financial obstacles to accessing care than adults in the ten other countries surveyed.

Many U.S. patients also say when they're sick they can't always see a doctor or nurse when they should. The Commonwealth Fund reported that 42 percent of Americans said the last time they needed medical care they did not see a doctor or nurse on the same or next day, and 51% said it was difficult to get care after hours.

Low-income patients are not served well; when sick they have difficulty accessing a doctor, and more than a third say they've waited six days or more to see one. In the previous two years half of low-income Americans had used the emergency department, the highest rate of any other country.

The baby boom generation is getting older now. While advances in medicine have allowed us all to live longer, they have also allowed us to live long enough to develop chronic diseases that are due in large measure to our lifestyle choices.

Rather than too-frequent doctor visits, higher spending is driven by greater use of medical technology, higher health care prices, and our inability to improve outcomes for those with chronic diseases.

But here's something to think about. While we would all agree that everyone should have access to affordable health care, and reports such as these are useful, is getting better access to our existing health care system the *only* solution to making Americans healthier? Or is there a dimension to health care that we're not addressing? The more you dig into the problem, the more you see that money alone is not the answer.

Americans Spend More on Health Care and Don't Get Healthier

Despite spending more on health care, Americans as a whole are not healthy. Americans have a shorter life expectancy and suffer from more chronic conditions than those in other first-world countries. Indeed, of all the world's nations, the United States ranks thirty-first in life expectancy. Countries that have longer life expectancies include Japan (number one in rank), Spain, Italy, Portugal, Greece, and even Slovenia.

Shockingly, the axiom that overall social progress and advances in medical science necessarily result in steady increases in human lifespan may not be true.

According to a Centers for Disease Control and Prevention (CDC) report released in December 2016, for the first time since 1993 life expectancy in the United States *dropped* significantly from the previous year. This was true for the entire population, not just certain groups. On average, Americans can now expect to live 78.8 years, a statistically significant drop from 78.9 years in 2015. Though this may seem to be statistically minor, it may portend a more significant continued decline in the future.

The report indicated the ten leading causes of death match the historical pattern, and in 2015 accounted for 74.2% of all deaths in the United States. For eight of the top ten leading causes of death, age-adjusted death rates *increased*, and many of these are preventable: heart disease, chronic lower respiratory diseases, unintentional injuries, stroke, Alzheimer's disease, diabetes, kidney disease, and suicide.

The age-adjusted death rate for cancer decreased, while the rate for influenza and pneumonia did not change.

Heart disease and cancer are still the leading killers of both men and women. Doctors continually preach to their patients the formula for how to drastically reduce their risk of developing either: eat right, exercise, and don't smoke.

Though it sounds simple, many people find it easier said than done. For all our spending, all our technology, and what seems like exceptional medical care, how can we possibly rank thirty-first in life expectancy? What's going on?

The Prescription Drug Epidemic

Following their training and current professional standards, many physicians try to solve their patients' problems with the tools available to them. As a result, doctors are prescribing more and more pills to help their patients with their symptoms. Hemant Mistry, a pharmaceutical industry analyst in Visiongain, said, "The incidence of diabetes will surge owing to rising levels of obesity and sedentary lifestyles in the global population."

In twenty-first-century America, doctors and patients are bombarded with a virtual tsunami of pharmaceuticals that focus on relieving symptoms. Again, symptoms demonstrated are not necessarily connected to the root cause—the emotional dimensions of health care. In 2011, approximately four billion prescriptions were issued all over the United States. The average annual number of prescriptions written per person is thirteen. At any given time, over one third of all Americans are taking a prescription drug. Nearly one half of all Americans age fifty-five and over take a prescription drug.

A particularly alarming trend is the startling increase in the number of opioid prescriptions—and deaths. From 2000 to 2010 the estimated total number of opioid analgesic prescriptions in the United States increased by 104%, from 43.8 million to 89.2 million, which meant that an astounding 11.8% of adults in America received a prescription for opioids during the year. Along with that increase came no demonstrable improvements in the health status of opioid users, but instead a growing number of opioid addicts. The Centers for Disease Control and Prevention found that drug overdose has become a serious national problem, with more people dying from drug overdoses in 2014 than in any previous year. Every day, seventy-eight Americans die from an opioid overdose. Overdoses from prescription opioid pain relievers are a significant factor in the fifteen-year increase in opioid overdose deaths. Sixty percent of drug overdose deaths can be linked to an opioid. And since 1999, overdose deaths involving opioids (including prescription opioid pain relievers and heroin) have nearly quadrupled in number.

An equally vital concern is the amount of prescription drugs being taken by children. As the *Wall Street Journal* reported in 2010, more than a quarter of US kids and teens are taking a medication on a chronic basis, and nearly 7 percent are on two or more such drugs.

Doctors and parents caution that prescribing medications to children must be done very carefully. Research is scant regarding possible effects of many drugs in kids. Health care providers and families need to carefully monitor and assess the impact of these medicines, both intended and as unintended side effects.

What's going on? How is it possible that the United States is pouring so much money into health care, and doctors are prescribing so many drugs and ordering so many tests, and yet the average American will live a life that is *shorter* than the average citizen of Slovenia?

The answer is much more simple than you might imagine.

The great thinkers in the health policy realm have tried to encapsulate an effort to fix our position in high spending with low return with the Triple Aim. The Triple Aim speaks to improve outcomes, improve patient experience, and lower costs, all of which are right minded and all of which need to be done. They are, however, incomplete as currently conceptualized.

As the most innovative continue to search for the golden ticket to beat chronic disease, some have even gone to the lengths of looking for retired football coaches, teachers, and other non–health care providers to become part of their team because these people know how to change behavior. My guess is they will be equally unsuccessful.

The underlying assumption on virtually all of these interventions is that to achieve better outcomes, patients need more information, reminders, and technical assistance. In fact, we have plenty of all three. Our friend Roy, from the story at the beginning of this chapter, is an upper-middle-class man with a good income and ready access to the health care system. Roy accepts his need for angioplasty following his heart attack, and his insurance will cover the majority of the expense. The resources he needs to fix a mechanical problem, like getting a heart valve installed, are at his fingertips.

But the *emotional dimensions* of recovery from Roy's heart attack are more elusive. Hospitals provide comprehensive written materials upon discharge and may recommend a support group. His provider may have an after-hours service that offers Roy verbal reassurance, and yet he returns to the emergency room repeatedly.

And while Janice is unemployed and struggling, she has a primary care physician who repeatedly offers patient education on healthy eating, refers her to weight loss programs, and holds her accountable at each visit with a weigh-in. Janice seems to know that repeatedly eating sweets makes her both *feel better* and *sicker*. She just can't bring herself to stop.

What is actually missing is the "why" in people's behavior. Clearly, a powerful force is working beneath the surface that drives people to make choices that, to a detached observer, seem to be irrational. The "why" in the concept of the emotional dimensions is *compensatory behavior*. Compensatory behavior is intended to relieve emotional distress, and both evolve along a continuum. This might be calling an ambulance because your think you are critically ill but the cause is anxiety or eating sweets to increase your feeling of well-being. The "why" from the perspectives of the emotional dimensions of health care is because the "bad" habit is actually "good" from the vantage point of the patient. Meaning it serves a purpose in their lives. With this pivot in thinking on our part, our health interventions on people's behalf need to understand the compensatory nature of these behaviors. Change will not occur no matter how hard one tries if the needs being met by that behavior are not addressed through new behaviors or substitutes (distress tolerance, coping skills, etc.). These "bad choices" have become so prevalent today that doctors have coined the term "lifestyle diseases," which result from the habits we develop rather than an underlying pathological process. This can never be only about a hard stop, going cold turkey, or willpower.

Health promotion advocates and doctors profess that changing our bad habits will make us *feel better*. But instead, while a successfully deleted bad habit will likely make the patient healthier, the loss of a functioning compensatory behavior will make them *feel worse* at a level that will quickly draw them back to the habit for relief. Simplistically trying to remove the bad habit that serves a purpose in the individual's life—the compensatory behavior—is a program destined to fail.

Chapter 2:

The Mind and Body Respond to Stress

We all want to feel better, but despite the billions of dollars spent and the millions of prescriptions written, we are neither healthier nor feeling better. Distress and the way we deal with it runs the gamut. It could be another Xanax to get you through the work day after a long and painful divorce, it could be eating carbohydrates even in the face of out-of-control diabetes to help manage the nightmares associated with your personal trauma, or it could be drinking daily to help you get through raising your children on a street wracked by violence.

This treatise is an attempt to articulate that as human beings we experience distress along a continuum of severity. This distress creates a need in each of us to compensate for the distress, often leading to behaviors, in this case compensatory behaviors. While our compensatory behaviors help us to go to work, care for our children, and maintain relationships in the short run, in the long run they create health problems. If the health care system is going to be able to effectively intervene and change these lifestyle choices, we need to have a series of interventions graded for intensity that mirror this continuum of emotional distress in the same way that traditional medicine would have progressively grading strategies based on level of pathology. America continues to underperform as Americans progress further along the continuum of emotional distress.

Why the poor performance?

Politicians and health care pundits point their fingers in various directions, or worse, deny that we even have a problem. None have a convincing answer.

I believe that our nation's continued struggle to achieve a better state of health is the result of consistently and repeatedly attacking the wrong problems.

Too often we treat the symptoms, leaving the underlying causes of disease untouched.

Don't get me wrong—there's a place for our high-tech medical miracles. The other day I watched on the news as two babies who were conjoined at the head were separated in an operation that lasted twenty-seven hours. Giving these two children a chance at a normal life was an amazing testament to our scientific and medical capabilities. Every day we see the incredible treatment given to wounded veterans who have lost multiple limbs, and we marvel at the progress made in designing and building prosthetic limbs. Bionic eyes, cancer gene analysis, a drug for hepatitis C, the ability to remotely read X-rays—the list goes on. These and many other examples highlight the enormous advances made by science and medicine in life-saving areas, and they are to be applauded.

We are truly living in an era of astonishing breakthroughs in medical technology.

But in many other areas of human disease we are not doing what we need to do, and as a result, too many people are suffering needlessly.

In framing our approach to curing disease, we too often ignore the effects of traumatic experiences and toxic stress—some of the best documented yet under-recognized and undervalued drivers of poor health outcomes, of health disparities in distressed communities, of unnecessary health care spending, and of profound human suffering.

An undeniable chain of causality links adverse experiences, unhealthy behaviors, our emotions, and our poor health outcomes.

To explore this chain, let's begin at the beginning.

The Science of Stress

Everyone loves to watch movies featuring tough-guy heroes like James Bond, who in the course of their work face hair-raising dangers that would crush ordinary people. In the darkened theater we relish seeing Bond get shot at, pummeled by bad guys, chased by all manner of lethal vehicles, dropped from airplanes, run over by speedboats, and blown up by bombs. At the end of each movie, the irrepressible Bond gets up, dusts himself off, and grabs the girl, and they happily drive off in a speedboat into the glittering sunset.

It's an amazing fantasy that James Bond can endure incredible stress and then bounce back as if he were made of Teflon. It's what makes the stories fun and allows the movie company to make sequel after sequel with the always-healthy secret agent ready to perform.

Alas, even people who aren't medical professionals know that such resiliency is the stuff of fiction. We know, either from personal experience or from knowing someone who has been affected, that stress and trauma, whether emotional or physical, doesn't quickly fade away after it's been removed. While incidental physical injuries may heal, the effects of stress and trauma often linger for years, and sometimes even a lifetime.

We all know this to be true intuitively. But what's the science? What do we know about the damaging effects of stress and injury?

Research indicates that adverse experiences and conditions trigger *real physical responses* from the body.

In order to discuss the possible effects of stress on the body, we need to first discover what the body does when it's put under stress.

A "stressor" can be anything that arouses a state of fear or apprehension. It can be a physical injury or the perceived threat of a future injury. For a cave man, it could have been the approach of a saber-toothed tiger or a prolonged drought. For a modern human, it could be getting robbed or losing a job. Long-term stressors might include living with an abusive parent, growing up in a high-crime neighborhood, or being chronically underemployed.

When a stressor presents itself, the human stress response system initiates a series of biological events, which scientists call the hypothalamic-pituitary-adrenal axis (HPA axis). Upon perceiving a stressor, a small area of the brain called the hypothalamus sends a chemical message to the pituitary gland. In turn, the pituitary releases a new chemical message into the bloodstream, which travels to the adrenal glands, located on top of the kidneys, which produce stress hormones. This message commands the adrenal glands to secrete cortisol.

Cortisol, a glucocorticoid (steroid hormone), is produced from cholesterol in the two adrenal glands. In all humans it's secreted at a predictable rhythm, called the circadian rhythm. Cortisol peaks early in the morning, then declines slowly over the course of the day to its low point, and eventually rises again in the early nighttime hours, slowly preparing for the morning peak again. Cortisol's systemic and widespread effects contribute to the body's effort to carry out its processes while maintaining homeostasis—or rather, as we are now discovering, allostasis.

Allostasis

In August 2016, Dr. Sandeep Jauhar wrote an opinion piece in the Sunday *New York Times* entitled "When Blood Pressure Is Political." He described a new theory emerging as an alternative to *homeostasis* in the body, which is the idea that the body's various systems strive to maintain an optimal and identifiable set point *at all of times*. For example, if your blood pressure drops acutely, in response your heart speeds up and the kidneys retain sodium and water, propelling blood pressure back to a customary set point.

In offering an alternative, Jauhar proposed that *allostasis* is not about preserving constancy; instead it's about continually fine-tuning the body's functions in response to external as well as internal conditions. This continuous calibration allows the body to fluctuate in response to changing demands, including those of one's social circumstances. Like a sailing ship constantly trimming its sails in response to changes in the wind, the body doesn't stay in a fixed state but rather adjusts its various systems in response to changing demands. These demands are not only physical; they may also be cultural, social, or economic.

The concept of allostasis relates directly to how the body regulates its various systems, including its production of hormones.

Humans typically experience two levels of stress hormones:

1. Resting (basal) cortisol levels. These are the normal everyday levels essential for normal functioning.

2. Reactive cortisol levels. These are increases in cortisol in response to stressors.

Here's what happens when the body is stressed: Stimulated by glucocorticoids and other stress hormones including adrenaline, the body and brain shift into what's commonly known as the fight-or-flight mode. The pulse rate and breathing quicken, sending more oxygen to the muscles. The blood sugar level rises. Bodily functions that are temporarily nonessential, including growth, digestion, and cell repair, are stopped. The person is in emergency mode, with mind alert and muscles ready for action.

When the crisis passes, the stress hormones normally recede to their previous, lower, baseline levels. But if the baseline levels of cortisol are *already* high, the body is on perpetual red alert and over time suffers more wear and tear.

The Center on the Developing Child at Harvard University described three kinds of stress effects on a child's body: positive, tolerable, and toxic.

Positive stress response is a healthy part of human biochemistry characterized by momentary increases in heart rate and mild elevations in hormone levels. Situations that might trigger a positive stress response are a ride on a roller coaster, the first day of school, or a visit to the doctor for an immunization.

Tolerable stress response triggers the body's fight-or-flight response to a heightened and more long-lasting degree. These deeper traumas may include experiencing a natural disaster, suffering the loss of a loved one, or being the victim of a crime. If the event is not repeated and is cushioned by positive relationships with adults who help the child cope, the brain and other organs return to a healthy state without long-term damaging effects.

Toxic stress response can occur when a child experiences prolonged, repeated, and/or intense adversity, including sustained exposure to violence, chronic neglect, physical or emotional abuse, caregiver substance abuse or mental illness, or the pressure of family economic hardship. A lack of adequate adult support will exacerbate the condition. Such long-term activation of the stress response systems can alter the development of the brain and other organ systems, increasing the likelihood of cognitive impairment and stress-related disease for years to come.

A persistently elevated level of glucocorticoid in the body can trigger Cushing's syndrome. Symptoms usually develop gradually, so the diagnosis may not be clear for some time. Some of the negative effects of Cushing's syndrome include obesity, with fat around the main body area rather than the arms and legs; diabetes; and high blood pressure.

Research on the biology of stress has shown that healthy childhood development can be disrupted by prolonged or excessive activation of stress response systems in the brain and body. Such toxic stress can have damaging effects on health, behavior, and learning that last a lifetime.

The effects of stress are not only felt by children; they can begin in the womb.

The exact role of stress hormones during pregnancy is nuanced, but prolonged, severe stress is known to be bad for pregnancy. The manifestation of stress is the production of maternal stress hormones. When stress hormone levels run high, women are less likely to conceive and more likely to miscarry. Babies born to stressed-out women are more likely to be premature and underweight. Such babies are more likely to experience developmental delays and metabolic diseases later in life.

As was reported in *Pediatrics* in January 2012 by Jack P. Shonkoff et al., although genetic factors play a role in an individual's response to stress, both environmental influences and childhood experiences can also have significant impact. Research indicates that beginning as early as the prenatal period, fetal exposure to maternal stress can influence the child's responsiveness to stress. The effect is not just limited to one generation; as Shonkoff et al. reported, in animals the effect has been displayed both in the offspring of the studied pregnancy and generations that follow. The authors write, "The precise biological mechanisms that explain these findings remain to be elucidated, but epigenetic modifications of DNA appear likely to play a role. Early postnatal experiences with adversity are also thought to affect future reactivity to stress, perhaps by altering the developing neural circuits controlling these neuroendocrine responses."

Stanford University biological psychology researcher Megan Gunnar and her colleagues conducted research with infants that confirmed animal research findings. They found that infants three months of age who received consistent, nonstressful care produced less cortisol. Babies at the age of eighteen months and classified as "insecurely attached" (i.e., who had received lower levels of nonstressful care) revealed elevated levels of stress hormone. At age two, these same children appeared more inhibited and fearful while continuing to display heightened levels of cortisol. Researchers had every reason to think these processes would apply throughout the lifespan.

Stress and the Immune System

For thousands of years, in the days before we knew about bacteria and viruses, people believed that stress itself could make you sick. Up until the science of disease emerged in the nineteenth century, the idea that the emotions were closely linked to disease was widely accepted. When people were ill, they were advised by their doctors to go to the water baths in Saratoga for mineral bath treatment or to bucolic resorts to relax in the fresh air. Gradually these ideas lost favor, the mind began to be viewed as a separate, self-contained organ, and the teachings of Freud took over as more well-defined causes and cures were found for illness. But recently, scientists like Dr. Esther Sternberg, director of the Integrative Neural Immune Program at the National Institute of Mental Health (NIMH), have been reaffirming the connections between the immune system and the brain.

The immune system is the body's defense against infectious organisms and other invaders. Through a process called the immune response, the immune system attacks substances and organisms that invade the body and cause disease.

The immune system is sensitive, and the body's condition can cause its strength to vary. Sleep is a factor, and sleep deprivation inhibits immune function, as do diseases such as diabetes and obesity. Poor diet, as well as the resulting trace mineral and nutrient deficiencies, can also diminish the immune response.

The immune response can be compromised by stress. As Andrew P. Ochtinsky of the Rochester Institute of Technology described, long-lasting psychological stress, including dealing with one's own terminal illness or that of a loved one, has been shown to reduce the effectiveness of the immune system, as has living in a distressed community. Performance stress, such as that of students during an examination period, has been shown to lower the response of the immune system to mitogen and to decrease disease-fighting cells. However, a person with a strong social support system tends to have stronger immune abilities. Even a positive attitude correlates strongly with helping the immune system to fight pathogens. This may sound like a simplistic "be happy, be healthy" self-help prescription, but recent research confirms that our attitude affects our behaviors, emotions, and health.

The immune system can be affected by stress-coping mechanisms. Relief of stress can dampen the immune-decreasing properties of strong negative emotions, which weaken immune response over time. People using cognitive-behavioral stress management therapies have demonstrated a more effective immune system. Why is this simple truth not an essential part of medicine today?

Stress has a direct, negative effect on the immune system by creating chronic inflammatory conditions and lowering the immunity of those who otherwise might have a healthy immune system. Individuals exposed to chronic social conflict experience high levels of stress and consequent impairment of the immune system, thereby increasing vulnerability to infectious and autoimmune disease.

The immune system can be affected by cortisol levels. Normally, during a response to stress, cortisol *suppresses* inflammation. But if cortisol is present in the blood for extended periods, the body develops a resistance to it and fails to respond to it properly. Instead, it increases production of substances that promote inflammation, called cytokines, leading to a state of chronic inflammation. Cytokines have been linked to a variety of chronic inflammatory conditions as well as autoimmune conditions, which occur when the body perceives its own cells to be a threat and attacks itself. Examples are lupus, fibromyalgia, and rheumatoid arthritis.

Hypertension

Earlier in this book I discussed the notion of allostasis and its impact on blood pressure. Sandeep Jauhar offered the example of hypertension, the term used to describe high blood pressure. This is a measurement of the force applied against the walls of your arteries as your heart circulates blood throughout your body. While high blood pressure usually does not cause visible symptoms, long-term high blood pressure is a significant causal agent for a host of diseases, including vision loss, stroke, coronary artery disease, peripheral vascular disease, heart failure, chronic kidney disease, and premature death.

Seventy million adults in the United States have hypertension. For more than 90 percent of them, the cause is unknown. However, we know that hypertension disproportionately affects black Americans, especially in poor communities. While there may be a genetic component, it's doubtful that this is a major factor, because black Americans suffer with hypertension at much higher rates than genetically similar black West Africans. Moreover, hypertension is common in other segments of society in which poverty and social ills are rampant.

Peter Sterling, a neurobiologist and a proponent of allostasis, has written that hypertension in these communities is a normal response to "chronic arousal," or long-term stress. In comfortable suburban communities, people aren't subjected to the same type of constant need for vigilance, estrangement from their neighbors, and conditions of poverty, racism, fractured families, and joblessness as they are in low-economic areas. While it may be true that money can't buy you happiness, it's clear that money can buy you relaxation, which alleviates chronic hypertension.

Where homeostasis attributes hypertension to a defect of regulation within the body's various systems, allostasis explains it as a *normal response* to social circumstances. Chronic arousal prompts release of stress-related hormones such as adrenaline and cortisol that tighten blood vessels and cause retention of salt. These in turn lead to long-term changes, including arterial wall thickening, which increase the blood pressure set point. The body then adapts to this higher pressure and works to maintain it.

As an example of such arousal, Dr. Sterling notes that blood pressure is often constant until about age six, and then it rises quickly as children become increasingly independent from their parents and strive to defend themselves against real or perceived threats. By age seventeen almost half of all boys demonstrate blood pressures in the prehypertensive range, while approximately 20 percent have full-blown hypertension.

In the allostatic formulation, no bodily system is presumed to be malfunctioning. Instead, unless shown otherwise, the body responds in the way it should to the chronic fight-or-flight circumstances in which it finds itself. The allostasis model identifies a seeming paradox: While people may be dying, their internal regulatory mechanisms are working as they should.

Stress Affects the Brain

Among individuals, the effects of stress can vary greatly. Some people seem little affected by it, while others experience significant negative responses. When we say that stress is "all in your mind," could this be literally true? Could the brain's response to stress be measured, and could we see damage to a brain that has been subjected to long-term stress?

The answer to all three questions seems to be yes.

Every day, people encounter stressful situations and stimuli. Stress comes in all forms, and some people cope with it better than others do, leading scientists to explore what this means. The National Institutes of Health studied identified brain patterns in humans, and the results indicate a condition of "resilient coping," which is the healthy behavioral and emotional responses to stress that allow some people to handle stressful situations better than others.

In a study of human volunteers at Yale University, scientists led by Rajita Sinha, PhD and Dongju Seo, PhD used a brain scanning technique called functional magnetic resonance imaging (fMRI). The system detects and measures how the brain responds during stress. Study participants were given fMRI scans while exposed to six minutes of stressful, violent, and threatening images, which were followed by six minutes of neutral, nonstressful images. During the scanning sessions, researchers also measured nonbrain indicators of stress among study participants, including levels of cortisol in the blood and their heart rate.

As compared to nonstress exposure, in response to stress the brain, when scanned, revealed a sequence of three distinct patterns:

1. Sustained activation of brain regions known to signal, monitor, and process potential threats.

2. An increase in the activation of a circuit linking brain areas involved in adaptation and stress response. The activation may have been a means of reducing the initial distress to a perceived threat. This activation was followed by deactivation.

3. Dr. Sinha and her colleagues described this as "neuroflexibility." It helped predict those who would regain emotional and behavioral control to stress. A feature of neuroflexibility is an early decreased activation of this circuit when first exposed to stress, which is then followed by its increased activation with sustained stress exposure.

"This seems to be the area of the brain which mobilizes to regain control over our response to stress," said Dr. Sinha.

The authors noted that previous research had consistently shown that chronic and repeated stress damages the connections, structure, and functions of the brain's prefrontal cortex, which is the seat of higher order functions, including language, attention, mood, and social behavior, and which promotes the regulation of emotions and the more "primitive" areas of the brain.

In the current research study, scientists found that participants under stress who did *not* exhibit the neuroflexibility response in the prefrontal cortex had elevated levels of self-reported maladaptive coping behaviors such as anger outbursts and binge drinking. Such individuals could be at increased risk for emotional dysfunction problems or alcohol use disorder, which are characteristics of prolonged exposure to elevated levels of stress. This, then, is the emotional dimension of health care.

Similarly, neuroscientists from the University of California at Berkeley reported in the February 11, 2014, issue of the journal *Molecular Psychiatry* that chronic stress triggers long-term changes in brain structure and function. Christopher Bergland reported on a series of experiments performed by Daniela Kaufer, UC Berkeley associate professor of integrative biology, in "Chronic Stress Can Damage Brain Structure and Connectivity." Kaufer and her colleagues discovered that chronic stress and elevated levels of cortisol can generate more overproduction of cells that produce myelin and fewer neurons than normal.

What's myelin?

It begins with the axon, a long, slender projection of a nerve cell, or neuron, that typically conducts electrical impulses away from the neuron's cell body. The axon transmits information to different glands, neurons, and muscles. Millions of axons create a network of fibers that interconnects neurons and creates a communications network between brain regions. This speeds the flow of electrical signals between neurons and brain regions.

Myelin is the white, fatty sheath that surrounds the axon. It's like insulation on a wire. In the 1870s, French physician Louis-Antoine Ranvier noted that the myelin sheath is discontinuous, covering most of the nerve fiber but with gaps at regular intervals along the axon. Scientists later learned that charged particles called ions can cross the axon only at these myelin gaps, which became known as the "nodes of Ranvier."

Scientists then found that this passage of ions helps maintain the electrical signal, allowing it to travel quickly down an axon. The signal appears to "jump" from one node to the next in a process called saltatory conduction.

For the axons and nodes of Ranvier to function properly, the distribution of myelin needs to be within a normal range. Too much myelin is just as bad as too little.

Cortisol is believed to create a cascading effect, establishing pathways between the amygdala and hippocampus to provoke the brain to be in a constant state of fight or flight.

Chronic stress has the ability to activate a switch in stem cells that turns them into cells that inhibit connections to the prefrontal cortex, impeding memory and learning, and lays down durable scaffolding linked to depression, anxiety, and post-traumatic stress disorder. According to the researchers, chronic stress decreases the number of stem cells that mature into neurons, and this might provide insight into how chronic stress also affects memory and learning.

Heart Disease

Numerous studies have shown that stress can promote tangible physiologic effects on the body, including the heart. This is particularly true in the case of severe and sudden stress. Under stress, the human body releases adrenaline, a hormone that temporarily causes the heart rate and breathing to accelerate and the blood pressure to rise. These responses prepare the body to deal with the situation and shift into the fight-or-flight response.

In some cases, people who've received traumatic news—like the death of a child—have suffered an immediate heart attack. "This isn't just an anxiety attack," said Dr. Deepak Bhatt, director of the Integrated Interventional Cardiovascular Program at Brigham and Women's Hospital, to *Harvard Health Publications.* "When you do a cardiac catheterization procedure on them, an artery that was previously open is now closed." The condition has often been called "broken heart syndrome," and it occurs more frequently in women, including those with no previous record of heart disease.

More research is needed to determine how stress contributes to heart disease, the leading killer of Americans. Researchers have found that stress triggers inflammation, which is a recognized component of many cases of heart disease. Yet stress may influence heart disease in more subtle ways. Stress clearly causes some people to act in ways that increase their risk for heart disease. For example, when they're stressed, people often compensate, consciously or not, by turning to comfort foods like pizza, doughnuts, and cookies; these high-cholesterol, high-fat foods exacerbate the artery damage that causes strokes and heart attacks. Stress can also intensify other heart-damaging behaviors, such as smoking and drinking too much alcohol. These habits can increase blood pressure and may damage artery walls.

Research studies also connect stress to changes in the way blood clots, which increases the risk of heart attack. If you are "scared stiff," not only does the intense fear seem to paralyze the body, it may even retard blood flow. Researchers at the University of Bonn discovered that when compared to the psychologically healthy population, people with an acute anxiety disorder are more likely to experience elevated levels of blood clotting. These results suggest that patients who suffer with anxiety issues will die from heart disease at a higher rate.

As was reported in *Science Daily*, in the system of human blood co-agulation, two mechanisms normally operate in opposite directions, each counterbalancing the other. On the one hand, *coagulation* refers to the blood thickening so that a clot can form and slow the rate of bleeding from damaged vessels. In contrast, *fibrinolysis* is a process that keeps the blood flowing easily and reduces clotting. In patients with anxiety disorders, researchers have reported an inhibition of fibrinolysis accompanied by an activation of coagulation. This is despite the fact that apart from the tiny prick for blood sampling, no injury had occurred. For these types of patients, the coagulation system didn't work properly as the coagulation tendency rose, with the likelihood of adverse consequences. In extreme cases, such an imbalance could produce a blockage of a coronary artery, leading to an emergency medical condition.

Myocardial infarction (MI), or heart attack, is the irreversible death (necrosis) of heart muscle as the result of a prolonged lack of oxygen supply (ischemia). It's estimated that in the United States, 1.5 million cases of MI occur annually. It's a serious health problem, heightened by the fact that approximately a third of patients suffer a sudden death without having shown any previous symptoms. Efforts to prevent infarctions before they occur have been the focus of research that investigates inciting events, or "triggers," of MI, arrhythmias, and sudden death. As J. S. Chi and R. A. Kloner reported in "Stress and Myocardial Infarction," it's well known that an MI can be triggered by an identifiable event, but research into cardiovascular triggers has only recently begun to identify specific causal agents. Research into triggering continues to make progress with deepening knowledge of the pathophysiological mechanisms involved in MI. The hope is that medical research can eventually develop effective preventive strategies.

It has been found that myocardial ischemia can be induced by routine activities of everyday life, including smoking and physical exertion, as well as a spectrum of negative emotions, including tension, anger, and sadness. Investigations into triggering have also extended into disasters, both man made and natural. Research studies have found rising rates of MI and sudden cardiac death following catastrophes such as war or an earthquake, indicating that emotional and psychological stress induced by external disasters can trigger cardiac events.

Chapter 3:

How Negative Social Determinants of Health Create Stressors

We've seen that a stressor can be anything that arouses a state of fear or apprehension. It can be an actual physical injury or the perceived threat of a future injury. When human beings are put under stress—whether physical or emotional—the effects are not simply unpleasant or inconvenient. Stressors often trigger measurable changes as the human stress response system initiates a series of biological events that can affect the heart, the immune system, the brain, and other bodily systems.

We have accepted that many of our life choices lead to chronic disease, which ironically leads to more stress and worsening health. Historically we have accepted the notion of "statistically expected" disease rates. In the absence of an interventional strategy to mitigate the stress that leads to the compensatory behaviors that lead to these diseases, we can continue to rely on those statistics.

For thousands of years, the question that humans have grappled with is, "What can we do to lessen disease and live longer?" In science, the question has revolved around those health factors that we can control. (Outside of science, people have tried all sorts of imaginative methods to forestall disease.) Science has long recognized that while some disease is considered statistically unavoidable—for example, it's a statistical certainty that at the end of your life your heart will stop beating—much of what ails us can be identified and influenced. We can kill bacteria, remove cancers, and even replace a damaged heart with one from a donor.

We can also make changes to our environment to promote better health, and if we cannot make changes in our physical environment, then we can change our emotional response.

The Social Determinants of Health

Much has been written of late around what are called the *social determinants* of health. What this means is how people's *life circumstances, both past and present*, directly affect their *present and future health status.*

It's a broad term that needs to be explained through a variety of lenses. Social determinants, as defined by the World Health Organization, are the conditions in which people are born, grow, live, work, and age. Distribution of money, power, and resources at global, national, and local levels shape these circumstances. These social factors determine most of the inequities in health—the unfair and avoidable differences in health status we see within and between countries. The truth is these affect us all in one way or another.

The US Office of Disease Prevention and Health Promotion, an office of the US Department of Health and Human Services, describes it this way:

"Social determinants of health are conditions in the environments in which people are born, live, learn, work, play, worship, and age that affect a wide range of health, functioning, and quality-of-life outcomes and risks. Conditions (e.g., social, economic, and physical) in these various environments and settings (e.g., school, church, workplace, and neighborhood) have been referred to as 'place.' In addition to the more material attributes of 'place,' the patterns of social engagement and sense of security and well-being are also affected by where people live."

But what is it about these situations that cause disease? The DHHS says, "Resources that enhance quality of life can have a significant influence on population health outcomes. Examples of these resources include safe and affordable housing, access to education, public safety, availability of healthy foods, local emergency/health services, and environments free of life-threatening toxins."

For the purposes of his book, I'm going to be a bit more precise and refer to *negative social determinants*. This is because if we were to specify, for example, that all social determinants were *positive*—a condition that could only exist in some sort of earthly utopia—then no stressors would be created and no disease would result. People might still get sick and die, but they'd die from accidents or from getting struck by lightning while in the backyard, and not as the result of adverse living conditions.

The Factors That Determine Our Health

Most people intuitively know that a variety of factors can make us either healthy or unhealthy. We know that smoking cigarettes is generally a bad health choice. We believe that if our mother had breast cancer, we might have a higher risk of getting it too. We assume that staying physically active is a healthier choice than being sedentary. But with the vast amount of health care information available to us—much of it highly dubious in its credibility—it's difficult for individuals, health care providers, and policymakers to know exactly how our health is influenced by the many powerful forces operating in the world around us.

How important for longevity, we ask, is our genetic family history?

How important is our environment?

How important are the dietary and lifestyle choices we make?

In 2002, J. Michael McGinnis, Pamela Williams-Russo, and James R. Knickman published their study entitled "The Case for More Active Policy Attention to Health Promotion," in which they addressed this key question by exploring the determinants of population health: genetic predispositions, social circumstances, environmental conditions, behavioral patterns, and medical care. Their research was driven by the fact that approximately 95 percent of the trillion dollars we spend as a nation on health care goes to direct medical care services, while just 5 percent is allocated to population wide approaches to health improvement.

They wanted to know if this lopsided approach made sense.

To begin their report, they discussed the five determinants, or domains, of health.

Genetics

Research suggests the apportioning of the genetic component is still uncertain. Although purely genetic diseases account for only about 2 percent of deaths in the United States, perhaps 60 percent of late-onset disorders, including cancer, diabetes, and cardiovascular disease, display a genetic component.

It's estimated that genetics plays a role in two-thirds of the risk of obesity, but, as with many similar predispositions, exposure to lifestyle factors that are controllable is a significant factor. For example, research into monozygotic (identical) twins with regard to the occurrence of schizophrenia, as well as similar twin research studies examining mental alertness in senior citizens, has revealed that about 50 percent of each could be explained by genetic factors.

While the BRCA1 gene accounts for only 5 to 10 percent of breast cancers in the United States, only 10 percent of colon cancers is attributable to a genetic source, and only about one case in twenty of elevated serum cholesterol levels may be explained by familial hyperlipidemia.

In their report, they apportioned to "genetic disposition" an overall share of 30 percent.

Social Determinants

Social determinants play a significant role in a person's overall health and longevity. As common sense might suggest, higher levels of wealth and education translate into better health and longer lives.

Living alone or with little human contact can affect your health. People lacking close social connections have a death rate two to five times higher than those who maintain close ties to family, friends, and community.

For example, researcher David Olds found that home visits by prenatal nurses to at-risk mothers reduced the rate of both risky health behavior and criminal activity up to fifteen years later.

Another significant influence is poverty, which has been estimated to account for 6 percent of US mortality. Research suggests that each 1 percent rise in income inequality (the income differential between rich and poor) may trigger a 4 percent increase in deaths among persons on the low end of the income spectrum.

In a 2016 study published in *JAMA Internal Medicine*, scientists at the National Institute on Aging (NIA) looked at the effects of race and economic status on mortality separately. They divided African-American men and women who were above and below the federal poverty line, and did the same for whites. They then compared their death rates over six years.

They found that African-American men who lived below the poverty line had nearly three times higher risk of dying early during the study period than those who were not poor. Among whites, the death rates were about the same for both economic groups. Among women, both African-American and white women living in poverty had a nearly twofold greater risk of dying early than their counterparts living above the poverty line.

Those results suggest that African-American men are particularly vulnerable to early death. The study did not make clear whether the causes were lifestyle, biology, or something else. But Dr. Michele Evans, deputy scientific director of NIA and one of the study's co-authors, told *Time* magazine the team will continue to study the population to isolate these factors.

"We are trying to understand what social determinants turn biologic processes in different directions and lead to differential longevity," she told reporter Alice Park. "As well as understand how they contribute to higher incidences of chronic diseases that occur much earlier in lower socioeconomic populations, particularly among minority Americans."

For the population as a whole, in any given year the most consistent predictor of the likelihood of death is the level of education. To put it simply, the higher level of education you have, the longer you're likely to live. People ages forty-five to sixty-four with the highest levels of education have death rates 2.5 times lower than those of persons in the lowest level.

As Patrick M. Krueger et al. wrote in their 2015 report "Mortality Attributable to Low Levels of Education in the United States," "Mortality attributable to low education is comparable in magnitude to mortality attributable to individuals being current rather than former smokers. Existing research suggests that a substantial part of the association between education and mortality is causal. Thus, policies that increase education could significantly reduce adult mortality." In their report, McGinnis, Williams-Russo, and Knickman gave "social circumstances" a 15 percent share.

Environmental Conditions

The places where people live and work can present hazards in the form of toxic agents, microbial agents, and structural hazards.

In our land, built structures, and water, a wide spectrum of environmental pollutants, toxic substances leaching from components of commercial products, occupational products, and chemical contaminants of water and food supplies have been associated with cancers, skin diseases, allergies, and other diseases of organ systems.

In the air, high levels of pollutants such as carbon monoxide, sulfur dioxide, and particulates have been associated with temporary increases in mortality and morbidity rates, in particular from cardiovascular and pulmonary conditions. Low estimates of the mortality cost of toxic-agent exposures are in the range of sixty thousand deaths per year.

Infectious disease threats can be traced to environmental conditions. In the United States, apart from behavior-associated diseases such as HIV and hepatitis B, many infectious diseases, given a hospitable habitat by environmental conditions, are significant contributors to early death. Each year, an estimated ninety thousand people die from infectious disease, not including those infections attributable to sexual behavior or use of illicit drugs, tobacco, or alcohol.

As we see over and over again, people living with negative social determinants often make choices that are risky but, on closer inspection, are in fact grounded in rational decision making. For example, in October 2016, residents of Flint, Michigan, already affected by the crisis of contaminated water, were burdened with a new complication to their lives: an outbreak of shigellosis, a bacterial illness that is easily transmitted when people do not wash their hands.

According to the Centers for Disease Control and Prevention, every year shigellosis affects 500,000 people in the United States. The disease is transmitted through the accidental ingestion of fecal matter containing the bacteria, such as when food handlers do not properly wash their hands. In theory, it's easy to control with thorough hand washing.

In Genesee County, where Flint is the largest city, health department officials reported an increase in the gastrointestinal illness, which can lead to serious diseases, including vomiting, fever, cramps, severe diarrhea, nausea, and stools containing mucus and blood.

In Flint, the decision by officials in 2014 to switch the city's water source from Lake Huron to the polluted Flint River destroyed consumers' trust in the city's water system. The bad water created health problems like hair loss and skin rashes, and triggered symptoms in children, including problems with coordination and weight loss.

Residents who were accustomed to drinking bottled water at home hesitated to use tap water for other household purposes, such as washing and cooking. They modified their personal hygiene habits, including where and how they took showers. Residents also began to use baby wipes, which they obtained free at bottled-water-distribution centers, to clean their hands. But because baby wipes are not chlorinated and do not kill the bacteria, this practice may have contributed to the surge in transmission of the shigella bacteria.

Other environmental factors such as worksite conditions, home hazards, and roadway design and lighting also exacerbate the burden of preventable injury morbidity and mortality. Every year, approximately seven thousand deaths occur from falls, fires, motor vehicle crashes, and work-related injuries linked to structural design and safety shortfalls.

McGinnis, Williams-Russo, and Knickman gave "environmental conditions" a 5 percent share.

Behavioral Choices

One of the more significant aspects of the emerging research on social determinants is the extraordinary role that our behavioral choices play in the development of chronic disease. When we talk about "lifestyle diseases," this is what it refers to. While ever more data supports the impact of behavioral choices, what is seemingly always left out of this analysis is the role that our emotions play.

These are the emotional dimensions of health.

In the opinion of Patrick Krueger et al., the single most prominent domain of influence over health prospects in the United States is our behavior patterns. These include our approach to safety; the substance abuse and addictions to which we succumb; the everyday choices we make with respect to diet, physical activity, and sex; and our coping strategies in confronting stress. They are all important determinants of health.

What we choose to eat and how we design activity into (or out of) our lives impact our health prospects. Dietary habits have been linked to diabetes, stroke, coronary heart disease, and cancers of the colon, breast, and prostate.

Physical inactivity correlates with an increased risk for life-shortening diseases, including diabetes, osteoporosis, heart disease, colon cancer, and dementia. In the United States, these diseases cause from 300,000 to more than 500,000 deaths annually.

Substance abuse and addiction take the lives of many Americans. Substance abuse as a whole represents the leading contributor of preventable illness, health costs, and related social problems facing U.S. families and communities today. As the Centers for Disease Control and Prevention reported, in 2014 drug overdose deaths in the United States hit record numbers, the most recent year of their survey. Up to 60 percent of drug overdose deaths involved an opioid. Since 1999, the number of overdose deaths involving opioids, including heroin and prescription opioid pain relievers, nearly quadrupled. From 2000 to 2014 nearly half a million people died from drug overdoses, and every day, seventy-eight Americans die from an opioid overdose.

For too many doctors, prescribing opioids, many of which were originally touted as being nonaddictive, has become an easy way to make patients feel better and relieve their pain. Sadly, a leading factor in the fifteen-year increase in opioid overdose deaths is overdoses from prescription opioid pain relievers. Given the large proportion of overdose deaths where the type of drug is not listed on the death certificate, these numbers may underestimate the true cost. The findings reveal two distinct but related forces pushing America's opioid overdose epidemic: a surge in illicit opioid overdoses chiefly as the result of the use of heroin and illegally made fentanyl, and a fifteen-year increase in deaths from prescription opioid overdoses. Both of these trends worsened in 2014.

The overall economic costs of addiction are estimated to be $428 billion a year in the United States, with addiction being a serious driver of health care costs, estimated at $215 billion annually. The economic burden of addiction in the United States is twice that of any other disease affecting the brain, including Alzheimer's.

In all, behavioral choices account for at least 900,000 deaths annually. Significantly, the behaviors Americans choose influence their health more than any other single factor.

In their report, McGinnis, Williams-Russo, and Knickman gave "behavioral patterns" a 40 percent share.

This left only 10 percent to the category of "health care." And yet this is where the vast majority of our national spending goes.

Negative Social Determinants of Health and Their Links to Stressors

Where do stressors come from? Are they related to negative social determinants? That is to say, while living in a high-crime neighborhood is generally recognized as a negative social determinant, can we say exactly *how* the high-crime environment creates a health problem?

We know that negative social determinants create stressors. For example, living in a high-crime area may mean that your chances of being physically injured—shot by a gun or having no heat in your house—are increased. It may also mean that your fight-or-flight hormones are chronically elevated, or that you seek to calm your nerves by getting drunk or eating fatty foods. In other words, the stressors created by the negative social determinant—living in a high-crime neighborhood—may impact you over a period of time, cause disease, and measurably shorten your life.

In looking at stressors more closely, we can identify four types that can affect your health.

1. Immediate physical injury. These injuries are obvious and well treated by Western medicine. They include broken bones, gunshot and other puncture wounds, and internal injuries from accidents. Generally, these are things that "happen to you," and unless you engage in risky behavior, like mountain climbing or joining a street gang in a big city, they cannot be avoided. You can go to a doctor and have such an injury repaired.

    However, if the injury was directly caused by a negative social determinant, such as a child harmed by his or her caregiver, then while the physical injury may be fixed, the emotional damage may remain for a lifetime. This persistent emotional damage may in turn create real and measurable health effects.

2. Chronic physical injury or condition. These are more difficult to cure or repair, and may last a lifetime. They include birth defects, severe war wounds such as the loss of a limb, or

blindness. The degree to which they affect the patient's sense
of well-being depends a lot on the patient's attitude.

3. Emotional stress, either transitory or long lasting. Common
sense dictates that a person living in a high-crime neighborhood
will experience a greater level of personal stress than someone
living in the suburbs who makes a comfortable living, because
their hormonal fight-or-flight response may be chronically
elevated. Other sources of personal stress include long-term
unemployment, an ugly divorce, getting laid off your job, or the
death of a loved one. The person who experiences this type of
stress may deny that it exists, either because they believe they
can't change it or because they sincerely don't recognize their
life conditions as being stressful.

4. Residual emotional stress from an event or events in the past.
These are often adverse childhood experiences (ACEs), which I
discuss in greater detail in the following pages. The key concept
is that while the event or events may have ended, the effects
persist. As in the previous type—stress from a challenging
environment—people who experience residual stress may deny
that it exists. A rape victim may want to "power through" her
terrible experience, or an adult who experienced violence at the
hand of their parent as a child may not link it to their current
malaise.

If some stressors don't involve a direct physical injury from an
outside source, then how does a stressor manifest itself in some other
way, such as through human behavior?

In several ways.

1. Self-inflicted injuries. These include smoking cigarettes, alcohol abuse, and use of dangerous narcotics. Traditionally, doctors and law enforcement have categorized these activities as choices made freely that can be stopped with enough willpower or, in the case of the use of illegal substances, a prison sentence. However, as we will reveal later in this book, while such choices seem to be freely made, and therefore represent what experts have long believed to be irrational choices, this may not be the case. It's entirely possible that under certain circumstances, a choice that leads to injury may in fact be a *rational* choice made to ease the pain from an underlying stressor.

2. Poor lifestyle choices. This category involves activities that to a certain degree are perfectly acceptable but which, when taken to excess, are harmful. Eating a donut is an acceptable activity, but eating a dozen donuts every day is unacceptable and may lead to diabetes. Watching the football game while sitting on your sofa is an acceptable activity, but sitting on your sofa for hours every day and never exercising is an unacceptable activity that will lead to obesity and heart disease. But as with self-inflicted injuries, these poor lifestyle choices may be rational responses to an underlying stressor.

There is even some new language emerging to describe what we might call self-generated health problems: lifestyle diseases. These are diseases borne of the decisions and

behaviors that we engage in rather than from some underlying, organic, pathological process. They are diseases of
wealthy nations that enjoy abundant access to food and
recreation. For example, in many Western countries people
consume high amounts of soft drinks, meat, sugary foods,
dairy products, vegetable oils, and alcoholic beverages. To
compound the problem, we're less physically active, and have
developed sedentary lifestyles and greater rates of obesity.
We also experience higher rates of colorectal cancer, breast
cancer, prostate cancer, endometrial cancer, and lung cancer.

It's not all related to wealth, however. In industrialized
nations, including the United States, lower-income adults can
develop lifestyle diseases through behavioral factors such as
unsafe living conditions, exposure to violence, unemployment
or underemployment, poor social environment, difficult working conditions, and stress, any of which can force someone to
change their lifestyle and personal habits that increase their
risk of developing one of these diseases.

3. Seemingly unrelated events and diseases. As in the case of
    Roy, the fifty-five-year-old married man from chapter 1 who
    appeared to be healthy but who had a heart attack, his out-
    ward malady may be the direct result of underlying stressors
    that his physician, using the tools available, may not uncover.
    For various reasons, both Roy and his physician may fail to
    "connect the dots" and see the big picture. Roy may deny that
    he's under stress; in fact, he may not even be consciously aware

of it. Or the source of stress may be removed, either in time (it happened in the past) or in distance (that is, Roy may be stressed at work but he doesn't want to bother his wife or his doctor, because successful men don't complain about such things). His physician may schedule the usual tests for Roy's heart, find nothing obvious, and then tell Roy to lose a few pounds and get more exercise.

Most perspectives on negative social determinants have to do with people living in extreme circumstances, whether that is children living with alcoholic parents, families living in poverty, or individuals living in highly distressed communities. More research today points to the irrefutable connection that social circumstances trigger a myriad of responses, including emotional distress, and that these responses take the form of rationally chosen *compensatory behavior* that can often result in poor health outcomes. This is all certainly true, and there is something we can do about it.

Research is showing that the previously mentioned concept of adverse childhood experiences (ACEs) can have repercussions that last a lifetime.

Adverse Childhood Experiences

Adverse childhood experiences (ACEs) are stressful or traumatic events, including abuse and neglect, that occur to someone at the age of eighteen or younger. They may also include nonphysical traumas such as witnessing domestic violence or growing up with family members who have substance use disorders. They aren't confined to those that appear in the headlines; potentially damaging events happen every day, both in public and behind closed doors, unnoticed by everyone except the persons directly affected.

Instead of being merely passing events that young people quickly put behind them, ACEs have been shown to influence the development and prevalence of a spectrum of health problems that can affect a person during their entire life, including those associated with substance misuse.

Common ACEs include:

- Physical, sexual, and emotional abuse
- Physical and emotional neglect
- Parent or caregiver treated violently
- Substance abuse within household
- A person in the household with a disruptive mental illness
- Parental separation or divorce
- A household member who is incarcerated
- A traumatic accident where someone is injured or killed

First published in 1998 in the *American Journal of Preventive Medicine*, the ACE study was conducted by Kaiser Permanente and the Centers for Disease Control and Prevention (CDC). It studied the short- and long-term impacts of childhood trauma on over seventeen thousand commercially insured members.

Having begun the project by trying to understand obesity, as the research unfolded they discovered something quite simple: Among adults with chronic health problems, many had high numbers of ACEs. These experiences were defined as witnessing violence, parental substance abuse, childhood neglect, and other, more catastrophic events.

The ACEs study found that 12.5% of the study participants had experienced four or more such events, and that there was a "strong dose response relationship between the number of childhood exposures and each of the ten risk factors for the leading cause of death." (The dose–response relationship, also called the exposure–response relationship, describes the effects seen within an organism caused by various levels of exposure, or *doses*, to a stressor after a certain exposure time. For example, if you *dose* a child with a stressful and violent domestic episode, there will be a corresponding *effect* on that child, which may last a lifetime.)

The risk for the following poor outcomes increased with the number of ACE exposures: smoking, alcohol and drug use, unsafe sexual behaviors, suicide attempts, fetal death, heart disease, depression, liver disease, obesity, and COPD.

This dose-response relationship brings us to the notion that there is a continuum of emotional distress that affects the choices we make, the lives we lead, and our basic health, both physically and psychologically. These experiences don't just happen to someone else. Fifty-nine percent of the men and women of America have at least one adverse childhood experience in their lives, and at least 10% experience five or more ACES. Seventy percent of teens in addiction treatment have a history of exposure to some form of trauma. Children with histories of any traumatic experience are twice as likely to have chronic health conditions as adults. Even the DNA in people with PTSD show increased levels of a gene that makes them more vulnerable to multiple types of sickness. This only strengthens our case to reduce the personal distress experienced by those exposed to trauma.

An adverse childhood experience need not be a sudden shock to the system.

In October 2016, Rivers Solomon, a novelist, wrote an opinion piece for *The New York Times* entitled "I Have Diabetes. Am I to Blame?" It's revealing not only for the insight she provides into the burden of having a chronic disease like diabetes but also for her heart-wrenching account of her childhood.

She was diagnosed with type 2 diabetes at the age of twenty-two. She wrote that people wondered if she had the sort of diabetes that happens for no reason, typically to young people, or if she had the sort that she brought on herself through what people perceive as a lack of willpower and self-control.

Culturally, this disease straddles the line between malignant and benign. On the one side, people obviously suffer from amputation, heart disease, blindness, and also from the side effects of constantly inflamed blood vessels. On the other, diabetics suffer from the invisibility of the deeply dedicated management it requires—diet, exercise, oral drugs, and insulin.

In type 2 diabetes, while the causes are not completely understood, some combination of genetic predisposition and environmental factors, including diet, exercise, and stress, cause the cells to demand more and more insulin to be able to take up sugar from the blood. As with most diseases and disorders, diabetes has a cascading effect on the body. Every chronic illness, disease, and disability carries with it misunderstandings. Solomon wrote, "I've found my fatness compounds this phenomenon. My body is visibly off kilter, a symbol for lethargy, lack of self-regulation, ill health, indolence. Combine this with the misbelief that there is a cure for diabetes—that cure being willpower—and everyone is suddenly an expert on how to fix me. It'd be impossible not to internalize that I am to blame. There is the issue of my blackness, too, which many, because of unconscious bias, interpret as inherently lazy, deviant, sick, unclean."

According to what she wrote, Rivers Solomon's adverse childhood experience was not one traumatic event but a long series of corrosive events over time. She wrote that she was teased and rejected for her body throughout her years in school. She wasn't fat as a child, but she was big. Extraordinarily tall for her age (four foot eleven inches in the first grade) and broad-shouldered, she saw the attention her grandmother lavished on her skinny cousin contrasted against the frustration she expressed shopping for clothes that fit Rivers. Her mother was kind and nonjudgmental, but when she visited her father over the summers, he put her on grueling diets, including one in which she was forbidden to eat solid foods before midday.

At the age of six, Rivers started dieting. Her mother briefly explained calories to her because it had come up in an unrelated conversation.

The next time she ate a slice of bread, she immediately got on her family treadmill until the number on the monitor denoting calories burned matched the number of calories per slice on the package.

In later years, she'd secretly drink sample bottles of perfume to try to make herself vomit.

She wrote that a lifetime of dieting and of being told her body was wrong had taken its toll, and she couldn't help conflating the messages that she was better off starved than fat. Maybe if she could let go of the shame, or more important, if the media, doctors, friends, and family could stop shaming her, managing her diabetes wouldn't be a roulette wheel of self-torture, and she could finally let go and heal.

The Broad Effects of Adverse Childhood Experiences

Adverse childhood experiences are not simply a construct designed to explain away adult health problems. If that were the case, the claimed cause and effect would seem contrived and limited. But it's neither, and in fact ACEs impact not just one's physical health but a wide range of behavior that's not directly related to someone being healthy or sick.

Consider the story told in 2016 by Jody Allard in *The Guardian*. Her article, entitled "I spent my life in debt. Now I know childhood trauma was to blame," is not a self-centered attempt to make excuses for bad choices but a reflection on a serious personal problem that resonates with truth.

Writing as an adult, she said that she couldn't remember a time when she had confidence in her ability to make sensible and responsible financial decisions. For years, she created for herself a record of poor credit and precarious finances. Like someone addicted to cigarettes, no matter how hard she tried, she could never seem to shake her bad habits.

She never considered herself to be good with money. In high school she had a checking account but thought little of writing bad checks to go to the movies or buy friends lunch. Following the same pattern, in college she was irresponsible with credit cards, maxing them out shortly after they arrived.

She easily blamed her circumstances for her poor money habits. After all, she had her first child at nineteen and had three by the age of twenty-one. Constantly broke, she suffered through shutoff notices and cupboards without food.

"But even when I worked my way into better jobs and should have been financially secure, I still couldn't seem to stop circling the financial drain. My kids had tons of brand name clothing and we lived in a beautiful home, but my bills were often sent to collections because I couldn't manage to pay them on time. On my 30th birthday, my car was repossessed after we got home from a nice dinner out."

She said that she earned more than enough money to make her car payments, and having her car repossessed was yet another rude awakening that left her feeling ashamed and embarrassed. Despite these experiences, she still didn't know how to get her finances under control. She told herself every day that she was irresponsible and bad with money, but it took her until her midthirties to finally ask herself why. She began to realize her financial instability was really just a symptom of a deeper problem. She didn't need more willpower or a fancy new budget app to get her finances under control.

She realized she needed to go to therapy, but not to learn how to manage her money. She *knew* she was terrible at balancing her checkbook. That wasn't the problem.

Until she went to therapy, she never connected the dots between the aftereffects of trauma and her lifetime of financial misconduct. As she wrote, "There aren't exactly billboards proclaiming the adult financial impacts of childhood abuse and rape."

Therapy helped her recognize how the lingering effects of trauma impacted every area of her life. Instead of having a multitude of problems, she had one big problem that worked in a multitude of ways. Her financial instability was a product of her emotional instability. Her recovery from trauma, which was a critical piece of her financial puzzle, depended on learning how to regulate her emotions without repressing or avoiding them.

She wrote, "As a child, one of my primary coping strategies was disassociation. I coped with financial problems by avoiding them or shutting down emotionally. Learning to view my financial mistakes as *childhood coping skills* gone awry, rather than ingrained character flaws, has helped me adopt more appropriate coping strategies."

Understanding why she made many of the financial mistakes she did helped her view herself not with shame but with compassion, and gave her the confidence to start rebuilding her credit.

Chapter 4:

The Continuum of Negative Social Determinants and Emotional Distress

A basic premise of this book is that stressors apply along a continuum of negative social determinants and emotional distress. We see evidence of an emerging recognition of this continuum of emotional distress with the number of stress reduction self-help books published, as well as documents like a recent periodical from Blue Cross Blue Shield (BC/BS) to their members outlining the importance of stress management in order to improve one's health. Similarly, we see a prevalence of support groups for people struggling with cancer or other life-threatening diseases.

If in fact our ability to manage distress in our lives is so fundamentally important to improving our health, why are we leaving it to self-help books and support groups? Particularly when we know that scientifically proven, evidence-based approaches are available to all of us. Whether our friend Roy or the broadly emerging notions of emotional eating have become commonplace language in weight management, medicine needs to become as focused and scientific in its approach to stress management as it has been in its diagnostic machinery and technological innovation.

These tools and techniques have names like emotional self-regulation skills, distress tolerance skills, and cognitive reframing. They are part of an array of human skills that can be taught and learned, and in fact have been for many years, but only for some. These tools evolved from the movement to develop psychotherapeutic approaches to improve the quality of life for those struggling with mental illness. Because of the earlier mentioned schism in medicine around the mind and the body and the profound and pervasive stigma associated with mental illness, we do not even consider these interventions as germane for the rest of us.

One of the enormous frustrations in the field of chronic disease management has been our collective failure to improve broad outcomes for people with chronic diseases. Over and over again, interventions focus on terms like health literacy and improved access to care. In our concept of the emotional drivers to so much of this compensatory behavior, these kinds of interventions are shallow and perhaps even disrespectful. In the same way that Daniel Goleman's concept of emotional intelligence is complementary to traditional notions of intelligence, chronic disease management cannot be good medicine without the emotional dimensions of health care. For example, as in the repeated weight gain–loss cycle for those struggling with obesity in spite of all of the technical programs, unless you get to the "why" of the behaviors rather than simply sharing the facts, they will inevitably fail in the long run.

Daniel Goleman has written extensively with great intellectual and commercial success around emotional intelligence and its relationship with *success in life*. In emotional dimensions of health, this book postulates comparable attention to the role our emotions play in our *health*.

Many efforts we see today and that we mentioned earlier, such as insurance companies paying for us to go to the gym, yoga, and the like, are positive signs. But unless we understand and act on the compensatory nature of our behavior, all of those signs become words without meaning.

As the health care industry continues to struggle with knowing how our emotions affect health, the emerging science of *behavioral economics* attempts to test and understand interventions that produce monetary rewards for individuals to change their behaviors in certain ways—for instance, in medication adherence rates. While such interventions have had modest success in the short term, the approach could in fact do more harm than good if, for monetary gain, people must give up the very things they think are keeping them productive and moving.

In this concept of a continuum of emotional distress, we must have a continuum of interventional strategies that parallel the levels of distress. The aforementioned BC/BS advice to their members to get rest, exercise, and eat well are probably fine for those who are having a bad day or week. But for those dealing with more significant and/ or chronic stressors ranging from responses to emotional eating to living in distressed communities and hearing gunshots at night, more sophisticated and intensive interventions are needed.

Indeed, negative social circumstances may be a leading cause of modern chronic disease. This is not to suggest that the allostatic formulation means that something is broken; the body responds in the way it should to chronic stress or the fight-or-flight circumstances it frequently finds itself.

What this means is that in situations where the body is put under stress, the driving force of allostasis will compel the body to make adjustments that, out of context, may appear irrational. We experience this as distress, and we want to do something about it.

The power of negative social determinants has been borne out by recent research. In 2010 the Millbank Memorial Fund conducted a large study of primary care, in which three of the most salient findings were:

1. Up to 70 percent of all visits to primary care sites stem from "psychosocial issues."

2. Although "patients routinely present with a physical complaint, the data suggests that underlying mental health or substance use issues are often triggering these visits."

3. When symptoms and trauma-related behaviors are left unaddressed, individuals often experience lower productivity, failed relationships, significant distress and dysfunction, difficulty caring for their children, and difficulty in caring for themselves in health-promoting ways.

In 2000, the National Council on Behavioral Health estimated that the cost of untreated trauma-related alcohol and drug abuse was $161 billion.

According to the National Association of State Mental Health Program Directors (NASMHPD), for people with serious mental illness on the far end of the continuum, this phenomenon is even more extreme. In fact, the prevalence of mental illness has created a perfect public health storm, with high rates of illness, both physical and psychological, and high rates of suffering, extremely high costs, and early death—some twenty-five years earlier than the average American.

Surprisingly, what we're exploring isn't new territory. Since the dawn of history and for thousands of years medical practitioners treated the person as a whole being, and diseases—rightly or wrongly—were attributed to all sorts of causes, both internal and external. Obviously much of this was dangerous nonsense, but beginning in the years after the First World War, when psychoanalytic theory came to the forefront of psychiatry, the field of medicine experienced an inexorable *separation* between the mind and the body. Doctors and scientists began to view the body as a sophisticated machine and that diseases of the body were presumed to be caused by an external source—a virus, bacterium, cold weather, poison. Disturbing events that happened to you were not relevant to your current state of physical health.

We now recognize that our emotions and the behaviors they drive are as fundamental to our health and well-being as our blood sugar levels or heart rate. In fact, a recent meta-analytic review of risk factors for mortality by Brigham Young University found that *loneliness* and *social isolation* carried the same risk for early death as did obesity.

The Long-Term Effects of Trauma on Mental Health

Research now shows that while stressors have an immediate effect on the mind and body, they also can have lingering emotional effects that can last a lifetime. In other words, the medical condition that you are battling today may in fact have its roots in a stress that afflicted you years in the past. Perhaps nowhere is this seen more acutely than in post-traumatic stress disorder (PTSD).

In 2011, W. D'Andrea and others, writing in "Physical Health Problems after Single Trauma Exposure: When Stress Takes Root in the Body," published in the *Journal of the American Psychiatric Nurses Association*, cited numerous examples of research studies indicating the lasting effects of a stress event.

They reported that one third of a sample of one thousand people have significant symptoms of PTSD at least ten years following a traumatic event.

When interviewed five years after their traumas, nearly one quarter of traffic accident victims had significant ongoing occupational and relational impairment, as well as clinically significant PTSD.

PTSD has been shown to be resistant to short-term treatment. A meta-analysis of the treatment of depression in people with early-life trauma histories established that treatment resistance in mood disorders is significantly higher. Likewise, in a meta-analysis of gold standard treatments for PTSD, researchers revealed that at least one third of people with PTSD do not respond to currently established interventions.

Other research focused on medical impairment documented by physicians. By virtue of the unfortunate and unforeseen terrorist attacks on 9/11, a national three-year longitudinal study by Holman et al., happened to capture its 2,729 participants before and after the attacks. The study revealed that physician-diagnosed cardiovascular ailments increased in the years following the attacks. Increases were also seen in respiratory, gastrointestinal, genitourinary, and musculo-skeletal conditions, all adjusted for age. Importantly, the majority of participants in this study did not have direct exposure to the attacks, which suggested that the physical ailment was not caused by personal experience of the attack, such as exposure to toxins.

Psoriasis and the Emotional State

Many people believe intuitively that a positive frame of mind—one relatively free of crippling emotional stressors—is associated with better health. A 2015 report by Cody J. Connor and others entitled "Exploring the Physiological Link between Psoriasis and Mood Disorders" discussed psoriasis, a chronic, immune-mediated skin condition. In addition to the adverse effects on patient quality of life of mood disorders like anxiety and depression, their findings suggested that such conditions can aggravate the severity of psoriatic disease. While the authors stated that the mechanisms behind this relationship are not clearly understood, a key causal agent between psoriasis and mood disorders seems to be inflammation; and "physiologic modulators of this inflammation, including the hypothalamic-pituitary-adrenal axis and sympathetic nervous system, demonstrate changes with psychopathology that may be contributory." They wrote that an imperative first step is the recognition of psychiatric comorbidity in treating these patients as a whole. The fact that psychological awareness can be critical to clinicians in their practice is underscored by the improvement in mood, which decreases the severity of psoriasis.

Stress may also cause unexplained itching. The risk of developing eczema, evidence suggests, is increased when a child under the age of two experiences the stress of a traumatic event such as a severe disease in a family member, or parental divorce or separation.

Therefore, in addition to prescribing the usual medication, a doctor treating a patient with recurring psoriasis might well be advised to determine the patient's emotional state to find out if hidden stressors could be aggravating the condition.

Gastrointestinal Diseases

The brain and intestines are controlled by many of the same hormones and parts of the nervous system. Research suggests that prolonged stress can disrupt the digestive system, irritating the large intestine and causing cramping, diarrhea, bloating, and constipation.

While it's now well established that *H. pylori* bacteria or the use of nonsteroidal anti-inflammatory (NSAID) medications such as aspirin and ibuprofen cause most peptic ulcers, research studies suggest that a person with *H. pylori* may be predisposed to ulcers by stress.

Irritable bowel syndrome, or spastic colon, is strongly related to stress. With this condition, the large intestine becomes irritated, and its muscular contractions are intermittent rather than wavelike and smooth. The abdomen can become bloated, and the patient experiences cramping along with alternating periods of diarrhea and constipation. Sleep disturbances due to stress can make irritable bowel syndrome even worse.

Changes Associated with Chronic Stress

As Zora Djuric and others reported in "Biomarkers of Psychological Stress in Health Disparities Research," while increased "production of cortisol and catecholamines enables humans to respond to real and perceived threats, excessive activation of the SAM and HPA axes has been associated with negative biological effects."

They point out that chronic stress is a risk factor for obesity, and cortisol increases the amount of abdominal or visceral fat, a component of obesity. Glucocorticoid excess damages the skin and muscles through reduced collagen production and atrophy, respectively, and also promotes osteoporosis via osteoblast inhibition. It also triggers apathy, depression, cognitive decline, and neuronal death in the hippocampus.

The long-term wear and tear, or allostatic load, caused by stress helps cause several diseases, including depression, diabetes, obesity, atherosclerosis, coronary heart disease, cognitive impairment, and both inflammatory and autoimmune disorders.

As Bruce McEwen wrote in his 2005 article "Stressed or Stressed Out: What Is the Difference?" published in the *Journal of Psychiatry and Neuroscience*, the allostatic load, which incurs wear and tear, can become an allostatic *overload* with the addition of external stressors. He wrote that the term "allostatic load" refers to "the cumulative results of an allostatic state (e.g., fat deposition in a bear preparing for winter, a bird preparing to migrate or a fish preparing to spawn)." These activities are part of the normal routines that animals use to obtain food and store additional energy for breeding, migration, molting, and other seasonal activities. These routines represent normal adaptive responses to seasonal and other demands. But if the animal experiences an additional load of unpredictable stressors, such as disease outbreaks, natural disasters, storms, or human interference, then the normal allostatic load can increase to become an unhealthy allostatic overload.

McEwen noted that to an acute challenge, "every system of the body responds, with allostasis leading to adaptation. When these acute responses are overused or inefficiently managed, allostatic overload results. Allostatic overload serves no useful purpose and predisposes the individual to disease."

For example, in response to an acutely threatening event, the brain secretes the stress hormones adrenaline and cortisol, which improve and promote the memory of the situation so that the individual can avoid similar situations. But if the stress is repeated, some neurons atrophy, resulting in *impaired* memory, while other neurons grow, enhancing fear.

Short-term acute stress *promotes* immune function by encouraging immune cells to invade areas in the body where they are needed to defend against a pathogen. Chronic stress does the opposite by using the same hormonal mediators to *suppress* immune function. As McEwen wrote, "For metabolism, glucocorticoids are useful in the short run by replenishing energy reserves after a period of activity, like running away from a predator. Glucocorticoids also act on the brain to increase appetite for food and to increase locomotor activity and food-seeking behavior." During periods of vigorous physical activity, this effect is *beneficial*. But the chronic elevation of glucocorticoids, which can occur as the result of chronic stress, poor sleep, or even an unhealthy diet, and which are then compounded by a lack of physical activity and low energy expenditure, can *block* glucose uptake by insulin. Whether an unhealthy diet, sleep deprivation, or a negative social determinant boosts high levels of glucocorticoids, allostatic overload can lead to insulin resistance and increased risk for cardiovascular disease.

The Emotional Effects of ACEs and Negative Social Determinants

While much of this book focuses on the impact of ACEs and negative social determinants on the physical health of a person—that is, the presence or absence of diagnosable disease treated by a doctor—these same forces can shape a person's life in ways that influence how a person is able to function as a productive member of society. It's a more elusive connection, but in many ways equally powerful. While someone like Roy, whom we met in the first chapter, has a heart condition linked to negative social determinants, in reality this condition could be just one of many different manifestations of an underlying stress. It's like looking at gophers on the prairie: you know they're under the earth and they're going to pop up somewhere, but you don't know exactly where. In Roy's case, the gopher popped up from the hole marked "heart disease." But with some slight variation in his life history and physical health, the gopher could have appeared at another hole.

Relationship Stress and Poor Health

Scientific evidence has long shown that the quality of a person's social relationships affects their health. As Debra Umberson and Jennifer Karas Montez wrote in "Social Relationships and Health: A Flashpoint for Health Policy," published in 2010 in the *Journal of Health and Social Behavior*, "Striking evidence comes from prospective research studies of mortality across industrialized nations, which consistently show that individuals with the lowest level of involvement in social relationships are more likely to die than those with greater involvement."

Umberson and Montez cited research that showed that the risk of death was double for adults with the fewest social ties as compared to those with the most social ties. Factors that might influence mortality, including health behaviors, socioeconomic status, and other variables, were taken into account.

Among adults with documented medical conditions, social ties also reduce mortality risk. For example, among adults with coronary artery disease, those who were socially isolated had a risk of subsequent cardiac death 2.4 times greater than those with more social connections.

The poor quality of a person's social relationships has been associated "with a host of conditions, including development and progression of cardiovascular disease, recurrent myocardial infarction, atherosclerosis, autonomic dysregulation, high blood pressure, cancer and delayed cancer recovery, and slower wound healing." Low quantity and poor quality of social ties have also been associated with factors associated with adverse health outcomes and mortality, including impaired immune function and inflammatory biomarkers.

A central source of emotional comfort for most people is their social relationships. However, stress can be caused by negative relationships. For example, while many individuals find emotional support in a good marriage, stressful marriages have been associated with depression and reduced endocrine and immune function. Marital strain can erode physical health, and advancing age can magnify the negative health effects of marital strain.

Through psychosocial, behavioral, and physiological pathways, relationship stress can undermine health. For example, stress in relationships can lead a person to adopt poor health habits in childhood, adolescence, and adulthood. Psychological distress and physiological arousal, including increased heart rate and blood pressure, are both influenced by stress, damaging health through long-term wear and tear on physiological systems. Such stressors also lead people of all ages to attempt to cope and reduce unpleasant arousal by engaging in unhealthy behaviors such as excessive food consumption, heavy drinking, and smoking.

Umberson and Montez wrote that over the course of one's life, the propensity to engage in particular risky health behaviors in response to stress can change. For example, in young adulthood stress is associated with more alcohol consumption, while in midlife it's linked to greater weight gain, presumably from comforting oneself with food. Relationship stress also negatively affects one's sense of mental health and personal control, both of which can be related to increased physical illness.

Social ties may have other types of unintended negative effects on health. For example, among diabetes patients, negative social environments and their perceived barriers predicted poor compliance to medical regimens. When one has an obese spouse or friend, our own obesity risk increases, and relationships with risk-taking peers contribute to increased alcohol consumption. This "social contagion" of negative health behaviors is manifested by several mechanisms, including perceived social norms. For example, friendship norms about dieting influence unhealthy weight control, and group drinking behavior influences alcohol consumption among young adults.

Personal health may suffer when caring for one's social ties. Caring for a sick or impaired spouse may trigger impaired immune function, poorer health behavior, increased physical and psychiatric morbidity, and declining health for the provider. Providing care to a sick or impaired spouse imposes stress that can undermine the health of the provider, even to the point of elevating mortality risk.

The recipient of care may also be negatively affected by interpersonal interactions with stressed caregivers. As they contend with the challenge of looking after aging parents, caring for spouses, and simultaneously rearing children, middle-aged people, particularly women, often experience high caregiving demands. In the future, the combination of an aging population and smaller families sharing in the caregiving of aging parents may mean that the multigenerational demands of social ties may become more pronounced.

Transitory Fear and Corrosive Anxiety

Fear is a funny thing.

On one hand, people love to experience temporary fear. They go to scary movies, jump out of airplanes, ride roller coasters, and otherwise subject themselves to episodes of pulse-pounding fear. They do this because they believe the fear will be short-lived and no harm will result.

On the other hand, true fear is a necessary survival mechanism. When you're walking in the woods and hear a "crack" of a twig behind you, and you turn and see a big hungry bear eyeing you, the fear that shoots through your body is a good thing because it means that you're switching to fight-or-flight mode.

Anxiety is different. Most people don't like to experience anxiety. It's a different kind of feeling, one that eats away at you. It's no fun and it doesn't do you any good.

To understand how the brain responds to a threat, it's important to know the physiological differences between fear and anxiety.

The story begins with the two amygdalae (singular: amygdala), almond-shaped groups of nuclei located deep and medially within the temporal lobes of the brain. They have been shown in research to perform a primary role in the processing of memory, decision making, and emotional reactions.

The triangle of neurons on the amygdala is called the lateral amygdala. It examines stimuli entering from the outside world, looking for threats. If it detects danger, then the neurons start firing, instructing the central amygdala to activate a defense response in the body. This process is not an emotion but a behavioral reaction and an unconscious physiological response leading to increased heart rate, perspiration, and shortness of breath.

The amygdala seems to have its own "memory" or imprint of childhood influences. As Barbara Ganzel and colleagues wrote in their 2011 article, "Allostasis and the Human Brain: Integrating Models of Stress from the Social and Life Sciences," how young adults as children perceived their parents' social status correlated to their amygdala reactivity in response to angry faces. This finding, which was independent of the subjects' ranking of their own perceived anxiety, demographic characteristics, social standing, depression, or personality traits, indicates that there may be long-term neural biomarkers of early social environment on emotional reactivity.

As Neil Strauss wrote in his 2016 article for *Rolling Stone* entitled "Why We're Living in the Age of Fear," fear is a powerful emotion.

When something threatening comes your way, you may have only one opportunity to do what you need to do to survive. You may not get a second chance.

"The more we learn about the brain, the more we learn it's not something that's supposed to make you happy all the time," reported Andrew Huberman, a neurobiology professor who studies fear at Stanford University. "It's mostly a stress-reactive machine. Its primary job is to keep us alive, which is why it's so easy to flip people into fear all the time."

The problem is that when we assess risk, we often have difficulty separating current reality from our stored memories and past responses.

According to neuroscientist Joseph LeDoux at New York University's Center for Neural Science, we experience fear in the conscious mind, the cerebral cortex. This is where we put together the experience and then label it as an emotion, or at least match it against other experiences that seem similar. Fear is created when the amygdala's emergency-response system is activated by a threat such as a dog snarling at you, or when the hypothalamus is alerted that a water-deprived body risks dehydration.

Where fear is a response to an immediate threat, anxiety is a response to something one anticipates *might be a threat in the future*. This sensation originates not in the amygdala but in a small area of the *stria terminalis*, the pathway linking the hypothalamus to the amygdala called the bed nucleus. Researchers believe it is this area that is overstimulated during social anxiety, post-traumatic stress disorder, and generalized anxiety disorder.

While fear is a response to a clear and present danger, anxiety is, in LeDoux's words, "an experience of uncertainty."

Living with these anxieties over a long period of time can, in two distinct ways, actually *change your brain.* The first is a physical change. "If you look at the cellular level of the prefrontal cortex and the hippocampus"—the thinking and memory-forming parts of the brain—"when you're living under constant states of fear and anxiety, you can actually see them shutting down," Justin Moscarello, who works in LeDoux's lab, told Strauss. "They shrink. They wither. And the amygdala actually gets bigger."

While this happens, functions including exploratory activity, logical thinking, and conscious decision making can be suppressed.

The second brain change is that anxiety of future danger can mutate into fear of present danger. Learning is a big part of threat detection, and when a benign stimulus activates the body's threat-response system, the overstressed brain can respond as if it's under attack. Recent research with rats demonstrated that when an electrical shock is paired with a tone, the rats become trained to exhibit a threat response to the tone alone. This is because selected brain chemicals become hard-wired to the fear response and link it to the tone.

Why does this matter? Because a person with chronic anxiety—including one who has suffered a significant adverse childhood experience—is likely to make personal choices with the intention of relieving their anxiety. These choices—drug use, eating sweets, or even behaving aggressively—may seem irrational until you look more deeply and reveal the underlying anxiety.

Chapter 5:

Americans Are Overworked, Lonely, and Getting Sicker

In this book we've talked about what we might call *active stressors*—things like adverse childhood experiences, diseases, and harsh living conditions. These are things that happen to you either once, repeatedly, or as a condition that lasts over time. Any one of the wide array of active stressors can trigger a stress response that can last a lifetime, leading to an allostatic overload and chronic ill health that does not respond to conventional medical approaches.

But can an allostatic overload be caused by *passive stressors*—that is, forces that act upon an individual silently, over time, without outward physical manifestation?

Increasingly, we're finding that the answer is yes.

Stress Can Be Spiritual, Too

While negative social determinants can be tangible, measurable things like living in a high-crime area, an adverse childhood event, or smoking cigarettes, there's increasing evidence—highlighted by the 2016 presidential election—that powerful stressors can be invisible.

On November 4, 2016, the Dalai Lama—the spiritual leader of Tibet—and Arthur C. Brooks, president of the American Enterprise Institute, collaborated on an opinion piece published in *The New York Times*. Entitled "Dalai Lama: Behind Our Anxiety, the Fear of Being Unneeded," the authors noted that in many ways there has never been a better time to be alive. Despite serious challenges in many parts of the world, in reality life has improved dramatically for billions of people. Fewer among us are starving, fewer are poor, fewer children are dying of treatable diseases, and literacy rates are higher than ever. In many countries, recognition of women's and minority rights has become part of everyday life.

And yet in many of the world's richest nations we see festering discontent. It's widely acknowledged that Donald Trump was elected president of the United States on a wave of voter anger and alienation. Why were people so angry? In the autumn of 2016, was the state of the nation really so terrible?

The answer, said the authors, comes from the fact that as human beings go about their business on earth, they need to not only stay alive, with their hearts beating and lungs breathing, but they need to *thrive*. People who are merely existing and not thriving suffer from diseases of the emotions, the body, or both.

As an example, they noted an experiment where researchers found that senior citizens who didn't feel like useful members of society were nearly three times as likely to die prematurely as those who did feel useful.

This spoke to a broader human truth: We all need to be needed. Feeling useless is a health stressor as dangerous as smoking or being obese. But having a sense of social self-worth does not equate with narcissism or having an unhealthy desire for the admiration of others. Rather, it consists of a natural human desire to serve our fellow citizens and help them improve their lives. It's the fundamental human trait of altruism.

Scientific surveys and recent research confirm the more we are connected with our fellow citizens, the better we feel. Selflessness and joy are intertwined. For example, in Germany, people who engage in social service are five times more likely to say they are very happy than those who do not view service as important. Likewise, Americans who believe in doing good for others are almost twice as likely to say they are very happy about their lives.

This helped explain, said the authors, why pain and resentment were spreading through prosperous countries. The problem was not a lack of material wealth. It was the growing number of people who felt they were no longer needed, no longer useful, and no longer one with their societies.

A feeling of being superfluous dampens the human spirit. In America today, compared with fifty years ago, three times as many working-age men are detached from the work force. Throughout the developed world this trend is increasing, and the consequences go beyond economic, leading to social isolation and emotional pain, and creating the conditions for negative emotions to flourish.

Unemployment, especially for men, can have significant health consequences. As Rick Nauert, PhD wrote in his 2015 article published in *Psych Central*, many men suffer more stress from not having a job than they do when they're employed.

In "Loss of Job Can Cause Premature Death in Men," Nauert described the project by Dr. Eran Shor, a sociologist from McGill University, who surveyed existing research covering twenty million people in fifteen (mainly Western) countries over the last forty years. Shor explored the effects of various stressful life disruptions on health and mortality in different countries and under varying conditions. These events include war-related stress, losing a loved one, work-related stress (including unemployment), marital disruption, and more. His research showed unemployment can shorten men's lives by an astounding 63 percent.

"Until now," Shor said, "one of the big questions in the literature has been about whether pre-existing health conditions, such as diabetes or heart problems, or behaviors such as smoking, drinking or drug use, lead to both unemployment and a greater risk of death."

In his work he reported finding that contrary to popular belief, preexisting health conditions had no effect, indicating a direct link between the stress of unemployment and poor health. Unemployment both causes stress and diminishes one's socioeconomic status, and unemployed people are likely to experience declining health and a higher mortality rate.

The risk of death is particularly high for those who are under the age of fifty. Moreover, investigators have found unemployment increases men's mortality risk more than it does women's—78 percent versus 37 percent, respectively.

Does the structure of a nation's health care system matter? No. In the US vs. Canadian vs. UK and others, the correlation between unemployment and a higher risk of death remained the same.

"We suspect that even today, not having a job is more stressful for men than for women," Shor said. "When a man loses his job, it still often means that the family will become poorer and suffer in various ways, which in turn can have a huge impact on a man's health by leading to increased smoking, drinking, or eating, and by reducing the availability of healthy nutrition and health care services."

In today's challenging economy, Shor noted, recently unemployed men may benefit from interventions aimed at reducing risk-taking behaviors as well as aggressive cardiovascular screening.

Getting laid off is not the only employment-related stress. Surprisingly, so is retirement. Researchers at Oregon State University found that healthy adults who stayed on the job and retired just one year past age sixty-five had an 11 percent lower risk of death from all causes, even factoring health, lifestyle, and demographic issues. Their findings showed that adults who described themselves as unhealthy were likely to live longer if they kept working, suggesting more than health alone affects mortality after retirement.

"It may not apply to everybody, but we think work brings people a lot of economic and social benefits that could impact the length of their lives," said lead author Chenkai Wu. Through the Healthy Retirement Study, Wu examined data collected from 1992 through

2010. The team divided the sample group into those who described themselves as "unhealthy" retirees (that is, people who reported that health was a factor in their decision to retire) and "healthy" retirees, who said that health was not a factor in their retirement. The healthy category constituted about two-thirds of the group, while the unhealthy category made up the remaining third.

"The healthy group is generally more advantaged in terms of education, wealth, health behaviors and lifestyle," said associate professor Robert Stawski, senior author of the paper, "but taking all of those issues into account, the pattern still remained. The findings seem to indicate that people who remain active and engaged gain a benefit from that.

"This is just the tip of the iceberg. We see the relationship between work and longevity, but we don't know everything about people's lives, health, and well-being after retirement that could be influencing their longevity."

America, Land of Anxiety

The relentless pursuit of happiness is a characteristically American struggle. The problem is that this elusive prize is creating a nation of nervous wrecks. According to the World Health Organization, despite being the richest nation on earth the United States is also the most anxious, and during their lifetimes nearly a third of Americans are likely to suffer from an anxiety problem.

But perhaps America's heightened levels of anxiety may not just be happening in spite of the great national drive to be happy, but also *because* of it.

The 2007 report by Ronald C. Kessler, PhD et al. entitled "Lifetime Prevalence and Age-of-onset Distributions of Mental Disorders in the World Health Organization's World Mental Health Survey Initiative" presented data on the lifetime prevalence, projected lifetime risk, and age-of-onset distributions of mental disorders in the World Health Organization (WHO)'s World Mental Health (WMH) Surveys.

In seventeen countries in Europe, Asia, Africa, the Americas, and the Middle East, researchers conducted face-to-face community surveys. They found that the estimated lifetime prevalence of having one or more of the disorders considered in the survey varied widely across the WMH surveys, from 47.4% in the United States to 12.0% in Nigeria. Symptoms consistent with the existence of one or more lifetime mental disorders were reported by more than one-third of respondents in five countries (United States, France, Ukraine, Colombia, and New Zealand), more than one-fourth in six (South Africa, Germany, Belgium, Mexico, Lebanon, and The Netherlands), and more than one-sixth in four (Spain, Italy, Israel, and Japan).

The WHO data did not consider schizophrenia, personality disorders, and eating disorders; according to the National Institute of Mental Health, in the United States the incidence of these disorders together is about 15 percent.

Nearly one in five Americans—currently, forty million adults—suffers from an anxiety disorder, the most common class of psychiatric ailment we have. Americans earn the top spot in being more anxious than anyone else, especially in their susceptibility to being nervous about the future.

According to the study, at some point during their lifetimes 31 percent of Americans are likely to suffer from an anxiety condition, as compared to 25.3 percent of people in Colombia and 24.6 percent in New Zealand, the countries that rank second and third. One might assume that people in developing or unstable states, where life is more precarious, would be more anxious than Americans. Not so. In reality, despite having to worry about life's basic necessities, people in developing countries such as Nigeria are up to five times *less* likely to show clinically significant anxiety levels than Americans. In addition, when these more relaxed citizens from the developing world emigrate to the United States, they are likely to become as anxious as Americans.

As Alice Walton wrote in *The Atlantic*, despite ongoing research, the predictors of mental health disorders are still evasive, even for the most common, like depression. While a nation's level of wealth would seem to have an influence on the mental health of its citizens, the data shows the relationship is more nuanced. Dr. Ronald Kessler, the Harvard researcher who headed much of the WHO's mental health research, reported that people in less developed countries tend to be less depressed: After all, he told Walton, "When you're literally trying to survive, who has time for depression?" On the other hand, Americans, who on average lead relatively comfortable lives, especially compared to people in Nigeria, far exceed other nations in the prevalence of depression, leading many to hypothesize that depression is a "luxury disorder."

What about the most drastic outcome of depression—suicide? In the United States every year, more than thirty thousand people die by their own hand, making it the eleventh leading cause of death in the United States. Across the globe, roughly a million people commit suicide each year, making it the fourteenth leading cause of death worldwide. Eastern Europe (particularly Lithuania, Belarus, Kazakhstan, Hungary), Russia, and Japan have the highest rates of suicide, while Peru, Brazil, Mexico, Colombia, and Israel have the lowest. The United States falls in the middle in its rate of suicide.

You'd think that if life in the United States were more stressful than other places, thus causing more disease, then the United States, as the world's richest nation, would be a leader in treatment. Not so. As Walton noted, in the US only 41.1 percent of people with mental health disorders receive treatment. In other parts of the world, treatment is highly correlated with the country's level of development and how much of the country's gross domestic product is spent on health care. Better treatment rates are generally seen in nations with universal health care, according to Kessler. In the US, he said, it's not the lowest socioeconomic class that has trouble. This is because they have access to Medicaid benefits, which usually cover at least some of the treatment. It's the second-lowest socioeconomic group that can't get care—they make enough money to be disqualified for subsidized health care, but not enough to afford quality care on the open market.

Anxiety disorders are the most prevalent mental disorders in the United States and among the most pervasive of all psychiatric disorders listed in the fourth edition of the *Diagnostic and Statistical Manual of Mental Disorders.* Greenberg and colleagues (1999) estimated that the annual societal cost of anxiety disorders exceeds $42 billion dollars. Likewise, Issakidis and colleagues (2004) estimated that caring for anxious patients costs $400 million.

While anxiety in America may be high now, do we know whether during the past several decades American anxiety has been decreasing, staying the same, or increasing? Evidence suggests that it's increasing.

Much of the richest data on this question comes from the Minnesota Multiphasic Personality Inventory (MMPI), which has been administered to high school and college students since the 1930s, and which includes many questions about symptoms. Among many other things, it asks whether respondents have trouble thinking, feel well rested when they wake up, and whether they have experienced symptoms such as shortness of breath, a racing heart, dizzy spells, or headaches.

Looking at MMPI questions over time, as a team led by Jean M. Twenge did in a 2009 paper in *Clinical Psychology Review,* a clear increase in symptoms associated with depression and anxiety emerges. Asked the same questions at about the same points in their lives, Americans say they are experiencing increasingly serious symptoms associated with anxiety and depression.

Quit Facebook, Get Happy

While this may seem trivial, for many people simply dislinking from the relentless pressure of peers on Facebook and other social media sites can ease an oppressive negative social determinant.

In his 2016 paper "The Facebook Experiment: Quitting Facebook Leads to Higher Levels of Well-Being" published in the journal *Cyberpsychology, Behavior, and Social Networking*, Danish sociologist Morten Tromholt proposed that staying off Facebook for a period of time has positive effects on two dimensions of well-being: our emotions become more positive and our life satisfaction increases.

Research has revealed these effects were significantly more pronounced among three types of Facebook users: heavy Facebook users, passive Facebook users, and users who tend to envy others on Facebook.

The results were based on a one-week experiment conducted in late 2015 in Denmark with 1,095 participants. The research compared the treatment group (participants who took a break from Facebook) with the control group (participants who kept using Facebook). The good news was that there was a bright side: Actively linking with a circle of friends, whether on Facebook or in real life, may actually increase one's sense of well-being.

According to Tromholt, improving peoples' well-being is both of interest for the people involved and society at large since well-being is said to be positively associated with other important aspects of peoples' lives, such as health and longevity. The study was undertaken because well-being research studies lacked causal evidence regarding the effects of social networks used in nonlaboratorial contexts. Facebook, being the most widespread social network of our time, was an obvious place to start investigating the consequences of social network use.

Tromholt cited another interesting study, one done by Christina Sagioglou and Tobias Greitemeyer, which found that when compared to twenty minutes of Internet browsing and twenty minutes offline activity ("control"), twenty minutes of active Facebook use ("treatment") led to immediate deterioration of the users' mood. According to the authors, the deterioration of mood was caused by a feeling of not having done anything meaningful. In addition, the study provided an interesting explanation as to why people keep using Facebook despite the network's negative influence: When logging into Facebook, the users expect the network to bring them positive feelings when, in fact, the opposite happens.

In their article "The Relationship Between Online Social Networking and Depression: A Systematic Review of Quantitative Studies" published in *Cyberpsychology, Behavior, and Social Networking*, David Baker and Dr. Guillermo Perez Algorta from Lancaster University asserted that you're more likely to experience feelings of depression when you compare yourself with others on Facebook than when you make social comparisons offline—that is, in the real world.

They examined recent research from fourteen countries with 35,000 participants aged fifteen to eighty-eight.

The Lancaster University research review found that the complex relationship between online social networking and depression may be associated with factors like gender and age. Comparing yourself with others can lead what researchers call "rumination," or overthinking, which in turn can bring on depression.

Short of unplugging from social media, can teenagers learn a coping mechanism to deal with all their stress and insecurity?

New research suggests adolescents can be taught practical skills to help them cope with the hazards of anxiety and depression.

A study by David S. Yeager, an assistant professor of psychology at the University of Texas at Austin, published in the journal *Psychological Science*, reported an effective new approach. At the beginning of the school year, ninth-grade students were given a reading and writing exercise designed to convey a basic, rudimentary lesson to help them manage tension: People can change.

As reported in *The New York Times*, when compared to a control group the students who completed the exercise reported more confidence in coping, had lower levels of stress, and achieved slightly higher grades at year's end. These results were measured through cardiovascular and hormone measurements as well as the students' self-reporting in online diaries.

John R. Weisz, a psychology professor at Harvard who was not involved in the research, found the approach efficient and powerful. "If you're an adolescent and you experience social harm, it's not fixed that you will always be a target. You can change," he said. "And over time, others can change, too. They may mellow and not be so cruel. That's an interesting twist for kids to learn, and a good one."

To date, Dr. Yeager and his colleagues have presented this intervention in five schools. In one study, three hundred high school freshmen participated in the exercise. Nine months later, they reported a rate of depression that was 40 percent less than in a control group.

If after the 2017 trials the results remain positive, Dr. Yeager has indicated he may release the intervention material through a project spearheaded by Stanford University designed to provide learning support for students.

The Stress of Loneliness

In their 2010 paper "Birth Cohort Increases in Psychopathology Among Young Americans, 1938–2007: A Cross-temporal Meta-analysis of the MMPI," Twenge and her colleagues found that the increase in anxiety in the American population may correlate to changes in how Americans relate to each other within their families and communities.

One change they found was that young Americans are increasingly focused on *extrinsic* goals. Between the 1970s and the present, surveys of high school and entering college students show increasing value placed on materialistic success, with more high school students agreeing that "having a lot of money" is important, and more college students agreeing it is important to "be well-off financially."

Expressions of narcissism, which is correlated with extrinsic goals, have also increased. (Is a self-created media celebrity Kim Kardashian a driver of the new narcissism or a reflection of it? Good question!) Young people also express significantly higher expectations regarding their careers and educational achievement. Some consider these expectations to be unrealistic because they aim far higher than is likely to be reality. At the same time extrinsic goals have increased, *intrinsic* goals have waned. Involvement in community groups rose between the 1930s and the early 1960s before falling sharply. Today, high school students are less likely to say they are interested in the affairs of government. When compared to 1985, in 2004 fewer Americans said they had close friends in whom they could confide. The divorce rate doubled between the 1930s and the 1970s (though it has since declined slightly), and the US Bureau of the Census reports that more people now live alone than ever before.

The intrinsic goal of "meaning" has also retreated, with lower numbers of college students agreeing with the statement that to "develop a meaningful philosophy of life" is important.

Twenge et al. conclude that the rise in psychopathology correlates with an increased amount of importance being placed on extrinsic goals such as material wealth, while less importance is placed on intrinsic goals such as affiliation. National economic cycles—periods of wealth and recessions—do not present significant correlation. The bottom line is that psychopathology increased among young people as American culture shifted toward emphasizing status, wealth,

and individual achievement rather than community and social relationships. Again, we see that social determinants—even if they
seem superficially positive—can have a detrimental effect on an
individual's health.

The authors conclude, "Over time, American culture has increasingly shifted toward an environment in which more and more young
people experience poor mental health and psychopathology, possibly
due to an increased focus on money, appearance, and status rather
than on community and close relationships." It's not hard to imagine
how this shift impacts not only wealthy people but those at the lower
end of the economic ladder, who may view their climb upward as
hopelessly Sisyphean.

Our Shrinking Social Networks

In their 2006 article "Social Isolation in America: Changes in Core
Discussion Networks over Two Decades," Miller McPherson, Lynn
Smith-Lovin, and Matthew E. Brashears asked whether the "core
discussion networks" of Americans had changed in the past two
decades. In other words, to what extent does each American have a
circle of friends and family in which they can confide, and has this
changed? The researchers returned to 1985, when the General Social
Survey (GSS) collected the first nationally representative data on the
close friends and colleagues with whom Americans discuss important
matters. In the 2004 GSS, the authors recreated those questions to
gauge social change in what they called "core network structures."

They found that among most Americans, discussion networks were smaller in 2004 than in 1985. The mean discussion network size decreased by about a third, from 2.94 in 1985 to 2.08 in 2004. This represented a loss of roughly one network person per American. Perhaps more alarmingly, the number of people saying there was *no one* with whom they discussed important matters nearly tripled. In 2004 the modal respondent reported having zero confidants; the modal respondent in 1985 had three confidants.

In the previous two decades both family and nonfamily confidants had been lost, but the greater decrease of nonfamily relationships led to more confidant networks focused on parents and spouses, with fewer connections made through neighborhoods and voluntary associations.

The authors asked why this question, and its disturbing answer, was significant. Social scientists know that contacts with other people are important in both socioemotional and instrumental domains. The stronger and closer our tie with another person, the broader the scope of their support for us; and in a crisis it's more likely they will provide help.

Most people have a network of interconnected confidants who are culturally or socially similar to them. Some changes reflect the changing demographics of the US population; for example, racial heterogeneity has increased while educational heterogeneity of social ties has decreased.

But what does our growing social isolation mean in terms of individual health? Is being socially isolated stressful, and can it make you sick? In their 2010 article "Social Relationships and Mortality Risk: A Meta-analytic Review," Julianne Holt-Lunstad, Timothy B. Smith, and J. Bradley Layton concluded that it could.

They noted that more and more people of all ages in developed countries are living not with traditional extended families but alone, and for these people a sense of loneliness is becoming increasingly common. As a survey by the Mental Health Foundation revealed, half the respondents in the United Kingdom agreed with the statement that people are generally becoming lonelier, a third say they have a close friend or relative whom they believe to be very lonely, and 10 percent often feel lonely themselves. Similarly, in the United States, the authors noted the threefold rise in the number of Americans who say they lack even a single close confidant.

Some experts have asserted that social isolation is a negative influence on human health. The authors highlighted a 1988 review of five prospective research studies that revealed people with more social relationships tend to live longer than those with fewer social relationships. While since that first review many prospective research studies of mortality have included measures of social relationships, the idea that a major risk factor for death is a *lack* of social relationships is still not widely accepted by either the public or health organizations.

In their study, Holt-Lunstad and her colleagues undertook a systematic review and meta-analysis of the relevant literature to determine the extent to which aspects of social relationships are most predictive of mortality, and which social relationships influence mortality risk. In other words, theirs was a study of 148 existing research studies.

Their findings indicate that the effect of adverse or missing social relationships on the mortality rate are comparable with well-known risk factors for death, including alcohol consumption and smoking, and *exceed* the effects of other risk factors such as obesity and physical inactivity. This is where we appear to be insufficiently informed. Whether in the doctor's office, media, or health promotion activities, we too often hear about the factors affecting our health while hearing little about the debilitating influence of missing or adverse social relationships. As evidenced above, we clearly have the data, and if we were to see it as relevant, the tools to begin addressing the emotional dimensions of health care are available to us. Stigma, the arbitrary distinctions between mind and body, and the particularly American "pull yourself up by your bootstraps" fix for things all create this blind spot in the medical establishment's efforts to improve our health.

The authors also assert that because many of the research studies used simple single-item measures of social isolation rather than a complex measurement, the overall effect of social relationships on mortality reported in their meta-analysis might be an underestimate. Although scientists need to perform further research to determine exactly how positive social relationships can be used to lower the risk of early mortality, they conclude that educators, health professionals, physicians, and the media should now acknowledge that social relationships can, and do, influence the health outcomes of adults. When discussing risk factors that affect mortality, we need to take a lack of positive social relationships as seriously as any other.

We're Overworked and Under-Vacationed

Polls reveal that a majority of Americans say they're stressed at work. One reason may be because they work more hours than workers in other industrialized nations.

According to a 1999 report by the International Labour Organization (ILO), an agency of the United Nations, Americans labored nearly two thousand working hours per capita in 1997, the equivalent of almost two working weeks more than their counterparts in second-placed Japan, where since 1980 the number of hours worked each year has been gradually declining.

The study examined eighteen key indicators of the labor market (KILM), including labor costs hours worked, underemployment, unemployment, and labor productivity. It showed that the American trend of increasing number of hours worked each year per person (which totaled 1,966 in 1997 versus 1,883 in 1980, an increase of nearly 4 percent) is going the opposite direction from recent worldwide trends in industrialized countries that have seen hours at work declining or remaining steady.

The long working hours of US and Japanese workers contrasts most sharply with those of European workers, who are taking more and more time off, particularly in the Scandinavian countries of Sweden and Norway, where hours worked in 1997 were, respectively, 1,552 and 1,399 per year—roughly 25 percent less than in America.

Working is good, but ever since the Bible Book of Genesis was written, we've been taught that periodically disengaging from our everyday routine can reduce stress. The problem is that too many Americans don't take advantage of their days off. A poll conducted by NPR, the Robert Wood Johnson Foundation, and the Harvard T.H. Chan School of Public Health found that about half of Americans who work more than fifty hours a week decline all or most of the vacation time they've earned.

In *Workplace and Health*, among respondents who actually take vacations, "Thirty percent say they do a significant amount of work while on vacation," said Robert Blendon, a professor and health policy analyst at the Harvard T.H. Chan School of Public Health who directed the survey. "So they're taking their stress along with them wherever they go."

Why do so many Americans have trouble leaving their job at the office? Many Americans who work fifty or more hours a week say they skip vacations because they want to get ahead at work. They say their office doesn't have many people with the same expertise who could serve as backup if they take days of, or there aren't enough people to pick up their workload.

Because time off can help alleviate stress and help the body ease back from an allostatic overload, it's an unfortunate trend that Americans are taking far less vacation time than they did a few decades ago. Recent research has revealed that employee health and well-being improve even during short getaways, which has prompted researchers who study workplace stress to urge people who feel they can't get away from the job for a week or two at one time to instead take long weekends throughout the year.

The findings of *Workplace and Health* revealed that a significant number of working adults say that their current job has a detrimental effect on their health. In particular, a significant share of working adults believe their current job affects their sleeping habits, family life, weight, social life, eating habits, stress level, and overall health. Almost half of all working adults say their workplace comes up short in its efforts to reduce their stress.

Workers who say they experience stress at much higher rates compared to other groups include those who:

- Work in low-paying jobs
- Are underemployed
- Face potentially dangerous situations on the job or who say there is something about their workplace they believe may be detrimental to their health
- Have ever cared for a sick family member while at the same time working a regular job
- Are chronically ill, have a disability, have fair or poor finances, work in restaurant jobs, and those working fifty or more hours per week in their main job

Furthermore, the report revealed that many workers have had the responsibility of caring for one or more family members who were injured, disabled, or seriously ill, while still needing to work at their current job. A majority of working adults say when they are sick they still go to work, and half of restaurant workers and more than half of workers in medical jobs say when they have the flu or a cold, they always or most of the time still go to work.

Put this all together and you get a picture of Americans who, despite living in the wealthiest nation in human history, don't see themselves as being particularly happy.

Gallup's Positive Experience Index actually seeks to measure national happiness levels. Each year the Gallup pollsters talk to people around the world; the 2015 poll results are based on telephone and face-to-face interviews with approximately one thousand adults in each of 143 countries, aged fifteen and older, conducted in 2014. The questions were:

"Did you feel well rested yesterday?"

"Were you treated with respect all day yesterday?"

"Did you smile or laugh a lot yesterday?"

"Did you learn or do something interesting yesterday?"

"Did you experience enjoyment yesterday?"

Despite its great wealth and democratic institutions, the United States did not come out on top. The highest "Positive Experience Index Score" of 89 was posted by Paraguay. The lowest score, 47, was claimed by Sudan, which by all accounts is a pretty miserable place to live.

The United States scored a middling 79.

For the first time in Gallup's ten-year history of global tracking, all of the top ten countries with the highest Positive Experience Index scores were in Latin America: Paraguay, Colombia, Ecuador, Guatemala, Honduras, Panama, Venezuela, Costa Rica, El Salvador, and Nicaragua.

In its summary of implications, the Gallup Organization quoted Robert Kennedy, who said, "The gross national product does not allow for the health of our children, the quality of their education, or the joy of their play . . . It measures neither our wit nor our courage; neither our wisdom nor our learning; neither our compassion nor our devotion to our country; it measures everything, in short, except that which makes life worthwhile."

Homelessness: Childhood Conditions Cause More Than Just Disease

While homelessness is not considered a physical disease, it's clearly a debilitating condition. While the condition of bring "homeless" is, at its most simplistic, one of not having a safe place to sleep at night that you control, it brings with it a host of adverse conditions that may include the increased risk of injury or illness; the challenge of constant hunger; potential harassment by the police, passersby, fellow homeless people, and criminals; exposure to the elements; and the never-ending threat of violence or personal injury. As a result of living in the streets, many suffer mental deterioration. All of these add up to a profoundly negative social determinant.

They are one of the most vulnerable and disadvantaged groups in the industrialized world, and their numbers are large—in North America and Western Europe it's estimated that at any given time more than one million people are without homes.

In trying to find the causes and solutions to homelessness, some good questions to ask are, "What type of person is likely to become homeless? Is it a matter of bad luck—getting laid off from your job and not being able to find another one—or is there something about the chronically homeless that makes rejoining the community difficult?" A number of research studies have found higher rates of serious mental disorders in homeless people, including personality disorders, depression, psychosis, and drug dependence. An obvious question is, "Are people likely to be homeless if they are already ill, or does being homeless make them ill?" Or is there a third possibility—that people who carry the burden of adverse childhood experiences are more likely to become homeless *and* more likely to be traumatized by the condition of homelessness?

In their 2014 article "Comorbidity of Attention Deficit Hyperactivity Disorder with Personality Disorders in Homeless People," Carlos Salavera and colleagues examined the relationship between homelessness and attention deficit hyperactivity disorder (ADHD). A development disorder with its origin in childhood, ADHD can persist in adulthood. Poor work and school performance are two functional anomalies associated with ADHD.

The goal of their study was to analyze the comorbidity of ADHD with axis II disorders in a homeless population in Spain.

They found that homeless people exhibit a rate of organic and mental disorders higher than in the population at large. They display personal, emotional, and social instabilities that influence both the diagnosis and prognosis of ADHD in childhood. There is a clear relationship between these two kinds of disorders, and among people with ADHD the prevalence of axis II disorders is higher than among the general population.

The researchers concluded that among homeless people, childhood ADHD often continues into adulthood, and there it's often seen together with personality disorders. In addition to the correlation between personality and psychological disorders, the homeless population showed a higher level of significant psychopathological symptoms, both in ADHD and the personality disorders, than did the general population. Homeless people often have difficulty in maintaining an adequate level of performance at work, achieving goals, and developing satisfactory interpersonal relationships.

These findings revealed how difficult it is for these subjects to establish and maintain steady social and personal relationships. The source of these difficulties may be the labor and academic problems displayed by people with ADHD, and may show the relationship between both pathologies.

As L. G. Murillo and colleagues noted in their article "Childhood Attention-Deficit/Hyperactivity Disorder Predicts Homelessness in Adulthood," among people diagnosed with ADHD in childhood, at age fifty-one the homelessness rate is 24 percent, far higher than in the general population.

They reported on a thirty-three-year prospective follow-up study of 207 boys of European descent diagnosed with ADHD at mean age eight years, with 178 controls matched for socioeconomic status and age.

At mean age forty-one, people with childhood ADHD cases were much more likely than others to be homeless for one week or more (24% vs. 4%). These results were controlled factors including for a conduct disorder developed by age eighteen, having dropped out of school, history of arrest, or having a nonalcohol substance use disorder (SUD).

Compelling evidence comes from someone who has firsthand experience with both ADHD and homelessness. A formerly homeless person, Derek M. Book is an outreach worker, case planner, and consultant living in Victoria, BC. Having earned his university degree, he's dedicated to the fight against homelessness and extreme poverty. He wrote on his blog "Formerly Homeless" that undiagnosed ADHD may be one of the largest causes of homelessness. "For many of us," he wrote, "homelessness is the only way to find peace from the relentless demands of systems and institutions. Some of us end up in jail, because it's actually a crime to not show up for court. We will house a homeless person who is dependable, who shows up to group therapy on time, who is predictable in behavior, but who can help the guy who 'made his own bed?' Most programs which help the homeless are merit-based, and ADD folks will never make the cut when so many others are competing for resources."

The key phrase is "homelessness is the only way to find peace from the relentless demands of systems and institutions." He's saying that for many adults with ADHD, homelessness is a *rational choice* that provides short-term comfort and lower stress. It's a way to achieve an allostatic balance, at least emotionally. While to a healthy person it may be incomprehensible that an adult ADHD sufferer would willingly trade physical comforts—a home, food, and safety—for the perils of the street, Book is saying that's precisely what happens. The emotional rewards—the removal of stress—are greater than the physical sacrifices.

Chapter 6:

How People Cope with Negative Social Determinants

It's an appealing dream to imagine that if only we made the effort, each and every one of us would have the power to change or improve ourselves and our immediate environment. Bookstores are overflowing with self-help manuals that offer pathways for personal improvement. According to these books and programs, with the right attitude you can leave your poverty behind and get rich. You can quit your lousy job flipping burgers, become a wealthy entrepreneur, and live in a mansion. You need only *think* about wealth and it will flow to you. By doing a specified activity you can lose weight or be happier or find inner peace.

From the Internet to seminars held at hotel function rooms, anyone who is burdened by a feeling of malaise can find plenty of advice on how to be happy and live a better life. You can let go of your stress, find the path that will give you financial and emotional freedom, and transform yourself from a stressed-out victim of modern society to a free person, poised to enjoy all that life has to offer. To overcome the deeply ingrained stress created by a lifetime of negative social determinants, you don't necessarily need a doctor; from the popular health industry, a typical prescription for the relief of stress goes something like this:

- Get enough sleep. When you're tired and sleep-deprived, you're more vulnerable to illness.
- Eat well-balanced meals. Keep healthful, energy-boosting snacks on hand. Avoid eating sugary or highly salted processed foods. Limit your consumption of soft drinks.
- Take time to unwind. Stepping back from a problem helps clear your head and put things in perspective. Listen to music, practice yoga, meditate, get a massage, or learn relaxation techniques. Or just go outside and take a walk around the block.
- Limit your consumption of alcohol and caffeine, which can aggravate anxiety and in some people can even trigger panic attacks.
- Exercise daily to help you feel good and maintain your health. Join a gym or start running every day. If you can't do that, then keep moving. At work, get up from your desk and walk around.
- Take deep breaths. Try doing breathing exercises where you inhale and exhale slowly. Count to ten, and as you do, imagine your stress dissolving. When you make a conscious effort to relax, problems that seem huge may become more manageable.
- Do what you can do and be happy with it. Instead of aiming for perfection, which isn't possible, be satisfied with how close you get. Set reasonable goals for yourself—not impossible ones, and not ones that are so easy that they're meaningless.

- Maintain a positive attitude. Make an effort to replace negative thoughts with positive ones. Too often, our flight-or-fight response is triggered by what we imagine is a threat to us and which may really be a minor problem.
- Talk to someone. Remember the research that found people who have a social network—friends and family they talk to—tend to be healthier and live longer. Tell friends and family when you're feeling overwhelmed, and let them know how they can help you. If necessary, consult a physician or therapist for professional help.

The suggestions go on and on, but you get the idea. The ideas are all easy to understand, clear, and quite rational.

In a perfectly mechanistic world, where each of us had full and complete control over every aspect of our existence, the solutions to our problems, including the stress from negative social determinants, would be as straightforward as these popular prescriptions. If we had a terrible memory of child abuse, we'd go to a therapist and talk it out. If the factory where we worked closed, we'd apply for a job somewhere else and get hired. If we smoked cigarettes, we'd either quit or take medication that eased the symptoms of withdrawal.

To the bafflement of experts in human improvement, people often ignore the obvious, rational choices for good health. Transforming a human life is a difficult task, and it doesn't always go as intended. If you live in a high-crime neighborhood, you can't just load up the car and move to the suburbs. If you're obese, it's extremely difficult to "just eat less." If your mother's boyfriend beat you when you were a child, the searing memory can't be erased the way you delete a file on your computer. If your fight-or-flight response is at its maximum because you're serving in combat in Iraq, you can't simply shut off the hormones when you board the plane to return home. As we've seen in this book, you've been hard-wired to be on full alert. Your brain and body chemistry can't easily return to a relaxed state but remain on perpetual high alert.

A stressed individual may reject rational solutions, or these solutions may simply be out of reach. If a solution to the problem of perpetual stress is not readily available, you might think that the response of the mind and body would be to do nothing. You might think the mind and body would in effect say, "There is no rational way to remove the stress that afflicts me; therefore, I'll simply accept it and do the best I can."

This does not always happen. The mind and body don't simply give up and end their resistance to the stressor that plagues them. In what must be an audacious mechanism for survival, the mind and body—often subconsciously—will take unorthodox measures to counterbalance the stressor, find emotional comfort, and by using allostasis, reach a workable equilibrium.

One way we see this is in self-medication. This is when an individual achieves allostasis through ad hoc methods of their own devising.

Self-Medication

The concept of self-medication has been a part of the thinking in the substance abuse world for many years. In academia, the idea that substance abuse can be a form of self-medication is formally known as the self-medication hypothesis, a term coined in the 1980s by Dr. Edward J. Khantzian, clinical professor of psychiatry at Harvard Medical Center. By the 1990s the term was used to describe how people use substances as a strategy of self-regulation, stemming from challenges in four different areas: self-esteem, emotions, interpersonal relationships, and self-care.

Not all soothing mechanisms come in a pill, and not every means of soothing the wounds that lie deep within us are prescribed by doctors. Common forms of self-medication include:

• **Food**. If you're an emotional eater, you might self-medicate with food. Emotional eating is when one uses food as a way to subdue or soothe negative emotions. "Comfort eating" may temporarily reduce stress in those who aren't clinically depressed. When we lose the capacity to regulate our inner stressors, or when too much uncontrollable stress makes it hard for us to find our own balance after an upset, we may turn to something outside of ourselves to soothe our frayed feelings. Just as over-the-counter medicine temporarily alleviates the symptoms of pain, so does the practice of self-medicating by emotional eating.

Research has revealed that overeating provides scientifically measurable short-term rewards. Not only does having
a belly stuffed with comfort food feel like a warm hug from
the inside, our brains give us a reward by releasing pleasure
chemicals similar to drugs and alcohol. Scientists studying
the blissful sensation after eating call it "ingestion analgesia,"
or pain relief from eating. The body rewards fatty, salty,
sugary foods by releasing endogenous opioids, which help
control pain. A study published in *Nature Neuroscience* suggested that cocaine and heroin affect the brain in much the
same way as high-fat, high-calorie foods. The study found
that when rats consume enough of these foods, they develop
compulsive eating habits that resemble drug addiction.

As the *Harvard Mental Health Letter* reported, the phrase
"stress eating" rings true. Stress, the hormones it releases,
and the effects of high-fat, sugary "comfort foods" drive
people toward overeating.

Ironically, short-term stress can shut down your appetite
because the hypothalamus produces a corticotropin-releasing
hormone that suppresses appetite. You have no time to eat
if you are running away! The brain also sends messages to
the adrenal glands to release the hormone epinephrine, also
known as adrenaline, which spurs the body's fight-or-flight
response.

But if stress persists, the adrenal glands release cortisol,
which increases appetite and boosts the motivation to eat.

Cortisol levels should fall when a stressful episode has passed, but if the stress doesn't go away, or if a person's stress response remains activated, cortisol may stay elevated. The release of cortisol appears to stimulate the storage of abdominal fat, perhaps a primary connection between stress and weight gain. Cortisol is a glucocorticoid, and this class of hormones, along with insulin, appears to trigger food cravings related to stress. Hormonally induced cravings for comfort foods, evidence suggests, may have a rational and biological benefit for managing stress. The negative hormonal and behavioral changes associated with stress may be alleviated by eating comfort foods, lessening the impact of stress on an individual.

Therefore, given no other easily accessible solution to the problem of stress, the afflicted individual may be *compelled* by his or her hormones to keep eating. This hormonally induced compulsion will make rational solutions such as dieting difficult because nothing has been done to manage the underlying stress that causes the oversupply of hormones that increase the appetite. Overeating needs to be viewed as a *symptom* of a disease, not as the disease itself.

• **Alcohol**. Many people can alleviate temporary pain by consuming alcohol and relaxing in the evening, say, or by knocking back some "liquid courage" before facing a daunting social event. In low doses, alcohol can temporarily relieve symptoms of depression.

Recent research examined the effects of alcohol on the amount of cortisol that is produced in the human body. As we've discussed earlier in this book, the body responds to stress through a hormone system called the hypothalamic-pituitary-adrenal (HPA) axis. When the HPA is stimulated, it secretes stress hormones, or glucocorticoids. Alcohol intoxication activates the HPA axis and results in elevated glucocorticoid levels, which, ironically, may add to the pleasurable effects of alcohol. But with chronic alcohol consumption, tolerance may build to alcohol's HPA axis-activating effects. Research studies have demonstrated that healthy young rats can develop tolerance to alcohol's stimulatory effects on glucocorticoid secretion—in other words, the rats produce smaller increases in glucocorticoid levels in response to chronic alcohol use. Pleasurable effects of the alcohol decrease, and the rats must drink more to achieve the same enjoyable sensation.

Post-traumatic stress disorder (PTSD) frequently results in self-medicating with alcohol. Research shows that trauma is often linked to alcohol use. According to the US Department of Veterans Affairs and the National Center for PTSD, up to 75 percent of those who have survived violent or abusive trauma report develop a drinking problem. Up to 30 percent of those who survive traumatic disasters, illness, or accidents report problems with drinking. For survivors who have ongoing health problems or pain, alcohol problems are more common.

• **Psychostimulants, such as cocaine and amphetamines.** People under stress often use psychostimulants to produce feelings of euphoria. Research has suggested that people with undiagnosed attention-deficit/hyperactivity disorder (ADHD) might self-medicate with cocaine as a means of placating inner tension. Cocaine has pharmacological properties in common with stimulants such as methylphenidate, which often is prescribed for ADHD. Cocaine and methylphenidate both alter brain chemistry with a similar mechanism of action, stimulating the buildup of dopamine in the nucleus accumbens, also known as the "reward center" of the brain.

• **Caffeine.** It is considered the most widely consumed psychoactive substance worldwide. It works in an unexpected way: the adenosine molecule tells the body that it hasn't had a sufficient amount of rest and is tired. To the body, adenosine and caffeine are almost identical, so the brain, which can't tell the difference, accepts the caffeine when it presents itself. The caffeine molecules then block the body's own adenosine from binding with brain cells and telling them the body is tired. So it doesn't give you energy; it simply tells the body to use what it's got.

• **Opiates and opioids, such as codeine, heroin, methadone.** The World Drug Report estimates that up to 32.4 million people worldwide use opiates and opioids annually. Depression is common among users of these drugs. Research suggests that people suffering from mood and anxiety disorders are more likely to use nonprescription opioids. Individuals self-medicate to reduce mood disorders, major depressive disorder, dysthymia, and panic disorder by using nonprescription opioids.

- **Cannabis**. It's the most widely used substance among those with depressive disorders. It has been found effective in treating depression in small doses, and is also used for pain relief.

Self-medication can also manifest itself as sex, gambling, or shopping. Some might even say social media and Internet use is a form of self-medication.

One of the main propositions of the self-medication hypothesis is that a person's choice of substances (e.g., heroin, cocaine, alcohol, prescription drugs) is closely linked to the particular negative emotional state that they are trying to manage. As Khantzian wrote in 1997, "The self-medication hypothesis of addictive disorders derives primarily from clinical observations of patients with substance use disorders. Individuals discover that the specific actions or effects of each class of drugs relieve or change a range of painful affect states."

He explained that self-medication factors occur in a context of "self-regulation vulnerabilities," which are difficulties in self-esteem, regulating affects, self-care, and relationships. People with substance use disorders often experience extreme emotions, and either seem not to feel their emotions at all or are overwhelmed with painful effects. As we have seen with so many other responses to either adverse childhood experiences or negative social determinants, substance abuse can be a rational choice because it helps such individuals to either experience or control emotions when they are absent or confusing, or smooth over painful effects.

If we begin to consider this notion of a continuum of emotional distress and negative emotions—sometimes beginning in childhood, sometimes from life events—creating a physiological response (as referenced by Dr. Jauhar), the most logical and normative thing people can do is to try to *compensate for that discomfort*. When facing the consequences of a traumatic event or of the effects of living in a highly distressed community, people naturally want to battle the deleterious feelings of stress, worry, and anxiety. Although individuals and groups have made innumerable efforts to combat the persistent disparities of health care outcomes in distressed communities, that's why they remain intractable. Most of those interventions frame the issue in terms of access to care and cultural competence. If we continue to ignore the *why* of people's behavior, whether it's overeating leading to diabetes or alcohol overconsumption leading to liver disease, we will never turn this issue around.

Binge Drinking

While it's hardly the only form of extreme self-medication, both binge and blackout drinking is widely documented and the topic of much discussion both in medical circles and at family dining room tables.

If you've seen the film *Animal House*, you might assume that binge drinking is confined to college campuses. In fact, as the National Institute on Alcohol Abuse and Alcoholism reported, binge drinking is a common form of self-medication in many social groups. According to the NIAAA, while college students commonly binge drink, so do adults; in fact, the vast majority—70 percent—of binge drinking episodes involve adults age twenty-six years and above. One in six US adults binge drinks about four times a month, consuming an average of eight drinks per binge. While binge drinking is more common among young adults, senior citizens (those aged sixty-five years and older) who are currently binge drinkers say they're binge drinking *more often*—an average of five to six times a month. Perhaps surprisingly, being in a comfortable income bracket doesn't matter; among people with household incomes of $75,000 or more, binge drinking is more prevalent than among those with lower incomes.

However, when young people drink, they often binge drink. About 90 percent of the alcohol consumed by youth under the age of twenty-one in the United States is in the form of binge drinks.

Perhaps most alarming is the report that more than half of the alcohol adults consume in the United States is in the form of binge drinking and blackout drinking.

What happens in the brain that causes a blackout and the accompanying amnesia?

In the brain, the hippocampus is a region integral to memory formation. Alcohol disrupts the receptors in the hippocampus responsible for transmitting glutamate, a compound that carries signals between neurons. As a result, some receptors are prevented from working, while others are activated. The neurons then create steroids, which prevent effective communication between the neurons, thus disrupting long-term potentiation (LTP), a process believed necessary for learning and memory.

What this means is the brain temporarily loses the ability to create new memories. While they're drinking, blackout sufferers still may be able to partake in spirited conversations or even—God forbid— attempt to drive themselves home. What they won't be able to do is create lasting memories during the time the alcohol in their blood was shutting down their memory-making abilities. Their immediate memories of what they just saw, heard, or felt are transitory, lasting only a few seconds until their attention is taken by something else they see, hear, or feel. They live in the past, with little present aware- ness and none of the future.

For the hours or even days the person is in a blackout state, they lose their awareness of who and where they are, as well as their most fundamental consciousness of self. It's like they're awake in a void, detached from time, unable to plan for the future, learn anything new, or form intent. They are unaware of what they are doing, not to mention why.

In 2016, Ashton Katherine Carrick, a student at University of North Carolina, Chapel Hill, wrote an article for *The New York Times* entitled "Drinking to Blackout." She described being a high school senior and visiting a prospective college. She was with a group of students who offered to give her a tour and let her spend the night in their dorm. The plan was to go to a fraternity party that night, and as a warm-up the group imbibed a concoction of booze that was blue in color.

"It's pretty stressful here during the week," explained the student who served up the blue concoction. "So everyone tends to go pretty hard on the weekends."

This was her first experience with the aspirational "blackout"—intentionally drinking with the goal of ingesting so much alcohol that your memory is obliterated and the only images you retain from the night before are the embarrassing videos your friends have posted to Instagram.

Carrick surmised that smaller colleges are especially susceptible to the development of blackout culture. Smaller colleges tend to be located in small towns with limited social activities. Thus, fraternity houses make up for the lack of bars and off-campus gathering places, to become the centers of social interaction and partying. She observed that drinking on campus was by far the easiest way to have fun, but it went beyond fun; some other element in the mix pushed them from casual drinking to binge drinking to blackout. As we have seen with so many other responses to either adverse childhood experiences or negative social determinants, it's self-medication taken to the extreme.

She thought it was the stress and an intense preoccupation with success. Rates of mental illness in young adults seem to be increasing. According to a 2013 survey by the American College Health Association, anxiety and depression are prevalent on America's college campuses, with 40 percent of male and 57 percent of female college students reporting feeling overwhelmingly anxious, while 27 percent of males and 33 percent of females said they felt seriously depressed. The association also found that since the 1950s, suicide rates in young adults had tripled, while the National Alliance on Mental Illness estimated that a quarter of college students have had suicidal thoughts.

Lifestyle Diseases

You may have heard the term lifestyle diseases and assumed it was a catch-all for the bad things that people living in wealthy industrialized societies do to themselves because of decadence, like the images of pampered citizens in the latter days of the Roman Empire lying around guzzling wine and eating grapes. The answer is twofold: yes and no. While the lifestyle diseases that we're currently experiencing may be more prominent in relatively wealthy societies, they're not necessarily the affliction of well-adjusted people who happen to live in a time of excess. The syndrome is much more complex and is directly tied to the emotional roots of illness. By the current definition, a lifestyle disease is a disease associated with the way a person or a group of people lives.

Lifestyle diseases generally include atherosclerosis, heart disease, and stroke; obesity and type 2 diabetes; and diseases associated with smoking and alcohol and drug abuse. They can be triggered and sustained by engaging in *health risk behaviors*. The Centers for Disease Control and Prevention (CDC) defines health risk behaviors as "unhealthy behaviors you can change." Four of these health risk behaviors—use of tobacco, lack of exercise or physical activity, drinking too much alcohol, and poor nutrition—are the cause of much of the suffering, illness, and early death associated with chronic diseases and conditions.

In 2011, more than half of US adults aged eighteen years or older did not meet the minimum healthy standards for physical activity or aerobic exercise. In addition, over three-quarters did not meet the recommended amount of muscle-strengthening physical activity.

Nearly half of US adults have one or more of these major risk factors for stroke or heart disease: currently smoking tobacco, uncontrolled high LDL cholesterol, or uncontrolled high blood pressure. Ninety percent of Americans consume too much sodium, increasing their risk of high blood pressure.

While in the United States the rate of cigarette smoking has steadily declined since the 1960s, in 2012, more than forty-two million adults—nearly 20 percent—said they currently smoked cigarettes. Each year, cigarette smoking accounts for more than 480,000 deaths, and each day more than 3,200 kids younger than eighteen try their first cigarette. Another 2,100 kids and young adults who occasionally smoke will become daily smokers.

Each year, overconsumption of alcohol accounts for 88,000 deaths, and experts say more than half of these deaths are the result of binge drinking. Perhaps surprisingly, while thirty-eight million US adults say they binge drink an average of four times a month, consuming an average of eight drinks per binge, most binge drinkers are not considered to be dependent on alcohol—that is, "alcoholics."

The effects are not limited to wealthy industrialized nations; lifestyle diseases afflict people at all points of the income spectrum, from the very poor to the most wealthy. As Mukesh Sharma and P. K. Majumdar wrote in "Occupational Lifestyle Diseases: An Emerging Issue," which focused on the Indian subcontinent, lifestyle diseases emerge when the daily habits of people have an "inappropriate relationship" with their environment. This means that from an objective viewpoint, the person is not living to optimize good health but is instead either *choosing* or is being *forced to adopt* habits that lead to poor health. The distinction is important. The person who has no choice but to live next to a polluted river and drink tainted water may be seen to have a lifestyle disease in much the same way as the person who lives in a mansion and drinks too many martinis.

The main factors contributing to lifestyle diseases, say Sharma and Majumdar, include incorrect body posture, poor eating habits, physical inactivity, and a disturbed biological clock. A report, jointly prepared by the World Health Organization (WHO) and the World Economic Forum, revealed that unhealthy lifestyles and poor diet cost India billions of dollars of economic losses. And worldwide, according to the report, in 2005 noncommunicable diseases caused 60% of all deaths (thirty-five million) and accounted for 44% of premature deaths. Even more concerning, in the future around 80% of these lifestyle deaths will occur in low and middle-income countries like India, which are also burdened by mounting nutritional deficiencies, infectious diseases, and poor maternal and perinatal conditions. They also noted a survey conducted in India by the Associated Chamber of Commerce and Industry (ASSOC-HAM) which found 68% of working women between the ages of twenty-one and fifty-two to be afflicted with lifestyle ailments, including chronic backache, obesity, hypertension, depression, and diabetes. The study, called "Preventive Health Care and Corporate Female Workforce," also said that when compared to women with lesser levels of psychological demand at work, the long hours and high-pressure deadlines cause up to 75% of working women to suffer from general anxiety disorder or depression.

In their 2013 paper "Co-Occurrence of Leading Lifestyle-Related Chronic Conditions Among Adults in the United States, 2002–2009," researchers Earl S. Ford, MD and others concluded that in the United States, "Public health and clinical strategies for meeting the emerging challenges of multiple chronic conditions must address the high prevalence of lifestyle-related causes . . . The prevalence of having one or more or two or more of the leading lifestyle-related chronic conditions increased steadily from 2002 to 2009." They wrote that if the trend continues, especially with teens and young adults, then treating patients in the aging population who have multiple chronic conditions will continue to be a high hurdle for clinical and public health practice.

They noted that in 2009 the five leading causes of death—diabetes, cerebrovascular disease, chronic lower respiratory disease, cancer, and heart disease—accounted for more than half of all deaths and represented a significant chunk of the nation's health care costs. In the United States, chronic diseases account for 75 percent of health care spending costs and more than 70 percent of deaths.

As Garry J. Egger and others noted in "The Emergence of 'Lifestyle Medicine' as a Structured Approach for Management of Chronic Disease," many lifestyle behaviors that cause chronic disease appear to be closely related in vicious cycles. The low-grade systemic inflammation now seen which is related to lifestyle diseases may be an underlying cause. They wrote, "Inadequate sleep, for example, can lead to fatigue; fatigue to inactivity; inactivity to poor nutrition or overeating; and all of these factors can exacerbate obesity and depression, leading to metabolic syndrome, type 2 diabetes, sexual dysfunction and mood problems, and potential heart disease." While the symptoms of many of these conditions can be relieved by medication, such treatment may also trigger serious side effects such as sexual dysfunction, exercise-induced myopathy, and weight gain. They assert that a thorough approach to the management of chronic disease would take into account a range of causal factors, including preceding events as well as expected risk factors.

Because lifestyle factors, including physical inactivity, smoking, alcohol consumption, poor diet, and overeating are the leading causes of morbidity and mortality, it is likely that, despite encouraging reductions in the rate of cigarette smoking, the continuing increases in high-risk lifestyle profiles could usher in an increase in the incidence, prevalence, and co-occurrence of chronic lifestyle-related conditions.

Battling the Rising Tide of Chronic and Acute Pain

As our lives become longer and presumably easier, our levels of personal pain, which you might think should be going down, seem to be going up.

According to a study prepared by National Institutes of Health's National Center for Complementary and Integrative Health (NCCIH), which appeared in *The Journal of Pain*, nearly fifty million American adults have significant chronic pain or severe pain.

The study, based on data from the 2012 National Health Interview Survey (NHIS), estimated that within a previous three-month period, twenty-five million US adults reported daily chronic pain, and twenty-three million more reported severe pain. People with serious pain suffer greater disability, and require and use more health care services than people with moderate pain.

In an NIH news release, Richard L. Nahin, PhD, MPH, lead epidemiologist for NCCIH and author of the analysis, said, "This report begins to answer calls for better national data on the nature and extent of the pain problem. The experience of pain is subjective. It's not surprising then that the data show varied responses to pain even in those with similar levels of pain. Continuing analyses of these data may help identify subpopulations that would benefit from additional pain treatment options."

Where does our pain come from?

As O. van Hecke, N. Torrance, and B. H. Smith wrote in "Chronic Pain Epidemiology and Its Clinical Relevance," the occurrence of pain, and particularly pain that interferes with daily life, can be influenced by a host of factors, including the occupational environment, employer and coworker reactions to pain, expectations, demands, the fear of reinjury at work, as well as broader issues including the health of the current job market. Many large surveys have shown that pain is more commonly reported by people with a history of abuse and violence at any age, in both domestic and public settings.

Recent NCHS data suggests substantial rates of pain from various common causes. The Institute of Medicine (US) Committee on Advancing Pain Research, Care, and Education reported in "Pain as a Public Health Challenge" that among Americans eighteen and older who, in 2009, reported pain, low back pain was most commonly reported. The most frequent single type of chronic pain was musculoskeletal pain, particularly joint and back pain; and most people with chronic pain had multiple sites of pain.

The US population has seen an increase in pain prevalence, and researchers say chronic pain rates are likely to continue to rise, for at least five reasons:

1. The rising rate of obesity correlates to chronic conditions that have painful symptoms, such as orthopedic problems (including cartilage degradation) and diabetes-associated neuropathy. Consequently, more Americans at younger ages will need to undergo joint replacement surgeries. These surgeries can cause acute and sometimes chronic pain that delays a full recovery and interferes with a full quality of life.

2. As the US population ages, a growing number of Americans will experience the diseases which contribute to chronic pain, including cancer, arthritis, cardiovascular disorders, and diabetes.

3. An undeniable risk of surgery is that of both acute and chronic pain as a result of the procedure. Patients may be discharged before health care providers have the opportunity to assess their level of pain, or they may be unable to carry out the prescribed pain management regimen at home.

4. Improvements in treating and saving the lives of people with catastrophic injuries related to military combat, vehicle crashes, sports, and work, or who in earlier times would have died, creates a growing cohort of relatively young people who may suffer lifelong chronic pain.

5. The development of new treatments and greater public understanding of chronic pain syndromes may cause people who previously gave up on treatment or who have never sought help to enter the health care system. In addition, people who gained access to health care coverage under the 2010 health care reform legislation may seek care for the first time, swelling the count of those who report chronic pain.

What are we doing about our pain?

Daniela Roditi and Michael E. Robinson wrote in "The Role of Psychological Interventions in the Management of Patients with Chronic Pain," published in 2011 in the *Journal of Psychology Research and*

Behavior Management, that patients will typically make an initial visit to a physician's office to pursue a cure or treatment for their ailment or acute pain. Despite medical and complementary interventions, some patients will find inadequate pain relief and will transition from an acute pain state to a state of chronic, intractable pain. Roditi and Robinson wrote, "As pain and its consequences continue to develop and manifest in diverse aspects of life, chronic pain may become primarily a biopsychosocial problem, whereby numerous biopsychosocial aspects may serve to perpetuate and maintain pain, thus continuing to negatively impact the lives of affected individuals." At this stage, the original plan of treatment may need to widen to include a psychological approach to pain management.

In the late 1960s, psychological approaches to managing chronic pain became increasingly popular with the emergence of Melzack and Wall's "gate-control theory of pain" and the subsequent "neuromatrix theory of pain." These theories proposed the idea that physiological and psychosocial processes interact to influence the perception, transmission, and evaluation of pain. They recognized the effect of these processes as "maintenance factors" intertwined with the conditions of prolonged or chronic pain.

The *biopsychosocial model* of pain may currently be the most widely accepted approach to understanding pain. This model considers chronic pain to be an illness rather than disease—that is, a subjective experience—and approaches to treatment focus on the *management*, rather than the *cure*, of chronic pain.

As the value of a more comprehensive and wide-ranging approach to the management of chronic pain emerges, interventions based on psychology are undergoing a notable rise in popularity and recognition as adjunct treatments.

Likewise, research on the effectiveness of interventions for chronic pain founded on psychology have shown some promising results on those key variables that have been studied.

Rather than eliminating the source of pain, current psychological approaches to the management of chronic pain try to promote cognitive change, behavioral change, and increased self-management. As such, they focus on the often-overlooked *behavioral, emotional,* and *cognitive* components of chronic pain as well as those factors supporting its maintenance.

A common and important—and yet often overlooked—underlying element of all treatment approaches is the taking into account of the patient's *expectation for treatment success.* While we've seen many significant advances in treating chronic pain, little attention has been given to the importance of the patient's expectations for success. Numerous research studies have confirmed that in the context of an expectation of relief, analgesic placebos can produce tangible and measurable changes in the perception of pain at a conscious self-reported level as well as a neurological pain-processing level.

Regrettably, health care providers often overlook the importance of patients' expectations as an important element that can contribute to the successful management of chronic pain. The trend in medical treatment is that even chronic pain ought to be managed through the "hard" technology of medical advancements rather than the "soft" technology of working with patient expectations.

Many patients who have become disillusioned with current treatment outcomes add to the drumbeat for finding the "cure." But with respect to chronic pain conditions, finding the cure has long been the exception rather than the rule.

Therapists have suggested that headaches, back tension and pain, shooting nerve pains, and muscle pain or fatigue can often be responses to unexpressed desires, needs, or emotions. They refer to this unconscious conversion of a mental state into physical symptoms as *somatization*. The presentation of somatic symptoms is a condition that can be diagnosed, as people with somatic symptom disorder (SSD) do not have imagined pain but actual physical pain, and their symptoms may be severe enough to affect work, relationships, and daily life. Stress and worry resulting from the symptoms tend to cause an individual's condition to worsen. An individual with SSD may wish to see a therapist as well as a health care provider in order to receive treatment for psychological symptoms as well as the physical ones.

As the current wave of chronic pain afflicts millions of Americans, a wise course would be to shift our approach from the elusive cure to the effective management of chronic pain. A practical path to achieving this is to educate pain patients as well as their circle of support on the best and most realistic expectations regarding the management of pain, and to capitalize on patients' positive and realistic expectations. A good place to start would be education regarding placebo and nonspecific treatment effects so that patients can let go of erroneous beliefs they may have previously held. Subsequently, health care providers can seek to enhance the expectations of their patients in a reality-based context and reduce negative expectations that stand in the way of successful treatment. When working with their patients, psychologists can introduce these topics and help their patients become more optimistic and better advocates of their own successful treatment.

Isn't that better than taking another pain pill?

Chapter 7:

Emotional Dimensions and Children

Having established that a body experiencing stress undergoes actual, measurable physiological changes, that these changes can persist long after the initial trauma, and that stressed people often choose to self-medicate to achieve a temporary allostasis, let's now return to a fundamental issue of this book, which is the importance of adverse childhood experiences (ACEs) in shaping our attitudes toward our own health and how we choose to maintain it.

Following is a key story that will serve as an illuminating touchstone.

The Adverse Childhood Experiences Study began in an obesity clinic on a nondescript street in San Diego. The year was 1985 and Dr. Vincent Felitti, chief of Kaiser Permanente's Department of Preventive Medicine, was mystified. He couldn't figure out why each year for the previous five years more than half of the people in his obesity clinic had dropped out. The program had been designed for the truly obese; although people who wanted to lose as few as thirty pounds could participate, the program was targeted for people who were up to six hundred pounds overweight.

The 50 percent dropout rate in the obesity clinic was puzzling. A cursory review of the dropouts' records revealed that all the participants had been *losing* weight, not gaining, when they had left the program. That made no sense whatsoever. Why would people who were three hundred pounds overweight lose one hundred pounds, only to quit when they were on the road to success?

Dr. Felitti decided to dig more deeply into the dropouts' medical records. His research revealed some surprises: All the dropouts had normal birth weights and had not gained weight gradually over several years; instead, most of them had gained weight abruptly before stabilizing. If they lost weight, over a short time they regained all of it or more.

He then conducted face-to-face interviews with several hundred of the dropouts. He used the same set of questions for everyone. For several weeks, the inquiries yielded nothing unusual, and he was no closer to figuring out the problem.

One day, Dr. Felitti was asking the usual series of questions to another obesity program patient: "How much did you weigh when you were born? How much did you weigh when you started first grade? How much did you weigh when you entered high school? How old were you when you became sexually active?"

"I misspoke," he later told the news website *ACESTooHigh*. "Instead of asking, 'How *old* were you when you were first sexually active,' I asked, 'How much did you *weigh* when you were first sexually active?'"

The patient, a woman, answered, "Forty pounds." She remembered she had weighed forty pounds when she had become sexually active. Then she tearfully added, "It was when I was four years old, with my father."

"I remember thinking," said Dr. Felitti, "that this was only the second incest case I'd had in twenty-three years of practice. I didn't know what to do with the information. About ten days later, I ran into the same thing. It was very disturbing." Suddenly, the floodgates seemed to open, and patients were talking about being the victims of sexual abuse as children.

Eventually, of the 286 people whom Dr. Felitti and his colleagues interviewed, most reported that they had been sexually abused as children.

But was there a direct link between childhood abuse and over-eating? The last piece of the puzzle fell into place when Dr. Felitti interviewed a woman who said she had been raped when she was twenty-three years old. In the year after the attack, she told Dr. Felitti that she'd gained over one hundred pounds.

"As she was thanking me for asking the question," said Dr. Felitti, "she looks down at the carpet, and mutters, 'Overweight is over-looked, and that's the way I need to be.'"

The revelation was that these obese people didn't consider their weight to be their primary *problem*; they saw it as an imperfect but absolutely rational *solution* to a condition of chronic stress brought on by an invasive, criminal attack.

In the paper "Why the Most Significant Factor in Predicting Chronic Disease May Be Childhood Trauma," published by The National Institute for the Clinical Application of Behavioral Medicine, Dr. Felitti discusses the meaning of this discovery.

The central question is how one gets from life experience in childhood to structural disease later in life.

The most direct path is through the adoption of selected coping mechanisms, of which overeating is one. Based on his experience in both successfully and unsuccessfully treating 30,000 obese patients, the challenge of obesity includes two core problems:

1. The use of food for emotional relief and psychoactive benefits. This is even built into our common vernacular: "Sit down; have something to eat. You'll feel better."

2. The presumed psychoactive "benefits" of obesity. This seems irrational, because isn't obesity a terrible health risk? Of course it is. The point is whether it serves a larger and more urgent purpose.

When doctors talk to their patients about this, it's quite remarkable what they can learn. Every week in Dr. Felitti's obesity program, for instance, he meets about thirty people who come to learn more about the program. Rather than describing the program to them, he gets right down to business and asks them some questions.

The first question is this: "Tell me *why* you think people get fat."

A woman answered, "People leave you alone."

He found that the key question in understanding the roots of obesity is this: "How old were you when you *first began* putting on weight?" Not "became obese," but "first began to overeat." There's a big difference, because most people take some time to become obese, and by that time the original reason—if there was one—is in the past. If there was a cause, obviously it had to be at the time they started overeating or shortly before. Dr. Felitti found that among people who had begun gaining in childhood, the number of times that those ages approximated parental loss through divorce was quite striking.

Just like physical or sexual abuse, divorce can be an adverse childhood experience.

There's no question that overeating may well be an effort at immediate coping or compensating, with the long-term health consequences appearing distant or less important. For example, no one smokes cigarettes to get lung cancer or heart disease; they smoke because of the pleasurable psychoactive benefits of nicotine. People ask, "Isn't it bad for you?" Of course it's bad for you—at some point in the future! But during those five blissful seconds of inhalation, when the nicotine surges to your brain, it has clear benefits. Nicotine plays an active part in terms of anger suppressant activity, appetite suppressant activity, antidepressant activity, and anti-anxiety activity. These factors have been delineated in medical literature for decades.

For many people, the common coping mechanisms are eating, smoking, drinking, and drugging. Alcohol is easy—you sit down, pop open a cold one, and relax. Street drugs are somewhat more complicated, at least to procure. Almost everyone knows the demonized street drug crystal meth is a big problem. But it pays to remember the first prescription antidepressant medication offered for sale in the United States was methamphetamine. In 1940 it was introduced by Burroughs Wellcome, and the brand name was Methedrine.

How could the first prescription antidepressant medication be exactly the same chemical as deadly crystal meth? Are people unwittingly buying antidepressants on the street? For the people in the American Rust Belt who are looking at a bleak future, the answer is probably, "Yes—crystal meth makes us *feel good.*"

Monisha's Story

In March 2011, Paul Tough wrote an incisive article for *The New Yorker* entitled "The Poverty Clinic." The story centered around a medical clinic run by Dr. Nadine Burke in San Francisco. One of her patients was a teenager named Monisha Sullivan.

Tough wrote that Monisha first visited the Bayview Child Health Center a few days before Christmas in 2008. She was a sixteen-year-old African-American teenage mother who had grown up in Bayview–Hunters Point, one of the poorest and most violent neighborhoods in San Francisco. Monisha Sullivan came to the clinic with symptoms that the staff often observed in patients: scabies, strep throat, weight problem, and asthma. After examining Monisha, Dr. Burke prescribed the customary remedies, including permethrin for her scabies, penicillin for her strep throat, and ProAir for her asthma.

At most clinics, Monisha would have been sent home. But as Dr. Burke diligently checked each box on the patient checklist, Monisha's problems appeared much more complex than her physical symptoms. The patient stared at the floor of the examination room and responded to Burke's questions in quiet monosyllables. Monisha was listless and depressed. She didn't like her foster mother, hated school, and seemed to have few feelings about her two-month-old daughter, Sarai.

Tough wrote that Dr. Burke took it upon herself to learn more about Monisha's childhood. She had been born prematurely, weighing just three and a half pounds, with a cocaine-addicted mother who had abandoned her in the hospital. Monisha grew up with a drug-abusing father and an older brother in a section of Hunters Point known for its gang violence. At the age of ten she and her brother were removed from their home and placed in separate foster care families. Since that time she had been shuffled through nine placements, staying with a family or in a group home until fights broke out and either her caregivers gave up or Monisha ran away.

Monisha suffered from nightmares, insomnia, and inexplicable body aches. When her hair started falling out, she wore a pale green headscarf to cover up the thinning area. Her hands sometimes shook uncontrollably. More than anything, she felt constantly and chronically anxious: about her daughter, school, even earthquakes.

Dr. Burke began to realize her patient's anxiety wasn't an emotional side effect of her difficult life. It was, in fact, the primary force influencing her overall health. According to Burke's research, the recurring adverse events that Monisha had experienced in childhood had triggered long-lasting and significant *chemical changes* in both her body and brain. These physical changes could be delivering a twofold punch: They could be both making her sick on a daily basis and multiplying the odds of serious medical problems in later years. Dr. Burke also realized that Monisha's case wasn't unusual; every day she was seeing in many of her patients similar patterns of stress, trauma, and symptoms.

"With someone like Monisha, we can help her recognize the neurochemical dysregulation that her childhood has produced in her," Dr. Burke told Paul Tough. "That will reduce her impulsivity, it will allow her to respond more calmly to provocation, it will help her make better choices. She'll have a better life."

Even with the knowledge of the powerful effects of ACEs, the road to recovery is long and hard. For many patients, especially the older ones, reversing the effects of years of adversity is difficult. In many ways, under the care of the Bayview clinic Monisha did quite well. Her asthma was brought under control, and she received a full set of immunizations. She graduated from high school, and in the fall enrolled in a San Francisco art school, taking classes in video production and theater.

Yet she suffered setbacks. School was a challenge and she was always short of money. She said an ex-boyfriend whom she had invited over one night because she was lonely assaulted her. Dr. Burke told *The New Yorker* she was realistic about the challenges that Monisha and other patients faced, and many days their problems felt overwhelming. Despite the daunting challenges, she was convinced that her new methodology would give patients a better chance at good health and a good future.

Social Media, Chronic Stress, Depression, and Anxiety

Among young people, the use of social media has become ubiquitous. Because of their undeveloped ability to self-regulate and the challenges of peer pressure, children and adolescents are at risk as they discover and experiment with social media. Real-world behaviors they must face include clique-forming, bullying, and sexual experimentation, which are increasingly connected to online problems like privacy issues, cyberbullying, and "sexting." Other problems teens face include sleep deprivation, social withdrawal, and Internet addiction.

For young people, seeking acceptance and being connected with their peer group are important elements of social life. However, the fast pace and vivid presentation of the online world, which encourages close and constant engagement, intensifies feelings of self-consciousness that may trigger depression in many people, both young and old.

Indeed, concerns over the effect of social media on mental health led the American Academy of Pediatrics in 2011 to define "Facebook depression" as a "depression that develops when preteens and teens spend a great deal of time on social media sites, such as Facebook, and then begin to exhibit classic symptoms of depression."

Not unlike offline depression, those who suffer from Facebook depression are at risk for social isolation. For help, they may turn to

risky Internet sites and blogs, which may promote unsafe sexual practices, substance abuse, and aggressive and self-destructive behaviors.

A study conducted by Professor Dr. Joanne Davila, her colleague
Lisa Starr, and Stony Brook University researchers revealed the link
between depression and social media. They discovered that, in a
sample group of teenage girls, a high level of Facebook usage correlated positively to a higher risk for depression and anxiety. A year
later, the researchers reevaluated the group for any signs of depression
or anxiety, and found something that seemed counterintuitive: higher
anxiety levels among those teens who frequently discussed their
problems with friends through social media as compared to those
who did not. According to Dr. Davilla, "Texting, instant messaging,
and social networking make it very easy for adolescents to become
even more anxious, which can lead to depression."

As a point of clarification, there's a difference between anxiety
and depression.

Someone with an anxiety disorder feels a sense of doubt and vulnerability about *future events*. They exhibit a variety of symptoms
that may include having anxious thoughts, unexplained physical
sensations, and self-protective or avoidant behaviors. They're focused
on their future prospects and the fear that those future prospects will
not be good.

In contrast, a person whose primary problem is depression, rather
than anxiety, generally feels that life is bad *right now*. They think
they already know what will happen, and they believe it's the same
bad stuff that's happening to them now. They're not so preoccupied

with worrying about what might happen to them in the future, and don't exhibit the same fear and uncertainty as people with anxiety disorders.

A girl who has anxiety fears that when she goes to a party her friends will mock her for her unflattering clothing. A girl who is depressed feels that her life is terrible at that moment.

In addition to being a source of depression and anxiety, social media can be a source of stress to its users. A survey performed on seven thousand mothers who were using the photo-sharing site Pinterest found that 42 percent of them said they suffered from "Pinterest stress."

Social media can cause depression and anxiety in two ways.

1. Chronic stress causes anxiety. To your instinctive fight-or-flight limbic system, being constantly on guard for new social media messages is the same as being on continuous alert for predators, which triggers the release of the stress hormone cortisol.

2. The social anxiety of stress is associated with trying to project a perfect self at all times. A person can suffer from high levels of stress by constantly trying to project an unachievable and unrealistic perception of perfection within their social network.

In their article, "Seeing Everyone Else's Highlight Reels: How Facebook Usage Is Linked to Depressive Symptoms" published in the *Journal of Social and Clinical Psychology*, Mai-Ly N. Steers and colleagues found that not only do Facebook and depressive symptoms appear at the same time, but a common factor is the established psychological phenomenon of "social comparison." That is, Facebook time and depressive symptoms are linked when we compare our ordinary moments to our friends' "highlight reels"—fun vacation images and cute baby pics. "You should feel good after using Facebook," Steers told *Forbes* magazine. "However, the unintended consequence is that if you compare yourself to your Facebook friends' 'highlight reels,' you may have a distorted view of their lives and feel that you don't measure up to them, which can result in depressive symptoms. If you're feeling bad rather than good after using Facebook excessively, it might be time to reevaluate and possibly step away from the keyboard."

For those who are already susceptible to depression, even the seemingly trivial depression caused by spending time on Facebook can have significant consequences. Because they are still learning to handle their own emotions, adolescents experience the problem most acutely. Research has shown that a single incident of depression during adolescence increases the risk fourfold of developing more serious depression later in life.

There is also question of whether using Facebook can increase the risk of depressed people harming themselves. To give its users tools for self-managing depression and its risks, Facebook has created a set of safeguards, including a suicide-prevention help page providing information on contacting a suicide hotline, and warning messages allowing viewers to report any suicidal messages they happen to read.

The safeguards aren't just for show. In 2014, eighteen-year-old Conrad Roy III committed suicide by inhaling carbon monoxide. Prosecutors claim that his long-distance girlfriend Michelle Carter sent Roy dozens of text messages encouraging him to follow through on his suicide plan. Roy and Carter met in person just once, in Florida in 2012, and for the next two years they conducted their relationship entirely over text messages. Roy had a history of issues with depression and had spent time in mental institutions, and had once told a girl he met in treatment that he was attempting suicide. She called 911, and his life was saved by emergency responders.

"He told his mother he 'would never do that to her again,' and never again mentioned wanting or trying to take his life to her," prosecutors wrote in a court filing.

On the day of his death, Roy spent the day walking the beach with his family and bought his sisters ice cream. He and his mother discussed his plan to attend the same college as his best friend and one day take over the family business. But while Roy spoke with his mother, he was simultaneously texting Carter about his plan to kill himself. Roy's mother told *New York* magazine he was distracted by his phone for much of the walk.

Finally, at four o'clock in the morning, Carter texted Roy, "You said you were gonna do it. Like I don't get why you aren't. So I guess you aren't gonna do it then. All that for nothing." Prosecutors charge that Roy might still be alive today if not for Carter's callous and persistent goading of a young man who, with the right treatment, could have lived a productive life.

The Alarming Rise in Teen Suicide

In the wealthiest nation in the history of the world, and one in which nearly 90 percent identify themselves as having a religious belief, the rate of suicide among young people is rising.

As Sabrina Tavernise wrote in her 2016 article "Young Adolescents as Likely to Die From Suicide as From Traffic Accidents," published in *The New York Times*, statistics reported by the Centers for Disease Control and Prevention reveal it's now equally likely for middle school students to die from suicide as from traffic accidents.

The CDC found that in 2014, the suicide rate for children ages ten to fourteen had surpassed the death rate for all accidents, including traffic accidents, which for decades had been the leading cause of death for that age group.

In fairness, the rate of accidental deaths has been dropping steadily for adolescents as well as adults. In 1999 the rate of accidental adolescent death was 4.5 per 100,000, and by 2014 it had fallen to 1.9 per 100,000.

Likewise, the rate of death by homicide, traditionally number three in rank, dropped from 1.2 per 100,000 to .8 in 2014.

These are both good developments.

The disturbing trend is that over the same period, the rate of death by suicide hovered around .9 per 100,000 until 2008, when it began to rise sharply to a rate of 2.1 per 100,000 in 2014.

"It's clear to me that the question of suicidal thoughts and behavior in this age group has certainly come up far more frequently in the last decade than it had in the previous decade," said Dr. Marsha Levy-Warren, a clinical psychologist in New York who works with adolescents, to *The New York Times*. "Cultural norms have changed tremendously from twenty years ago."

Why the sudden upsurge?

No single factor causes suicide, and its underlying causes are complex. But there's no doubt that social media can intensify the insecurities and challenges girls are experiencing at that age, possibly heightening risks, adolescent health experts said.

At the risk of sounding simplistic, it would be useful to note that Facebook made its debut in 2004, and by August 2008 had reached one hundred million users. By 2014 the number of users had grown to nearly 1.4 billion worldwide.

Instagram was launched in October 2010. By February 2013 it boasted one hundred million users.

Statistically, girls are the majority users of social sites like Instagram and Facebook, where they receive instant validation—or condemnation—from their peers. Such sites provide a way to measure personal popularity, and take thoughts and feelings that used to be private and abstract and make them public and concrete.

A negative peer response can be especially painful. Social media amplifies humiliation, and a sensitive or vulnerable young person who is shamed is at a heightened risk of suicide.

"If something gets said that's hurtful or humiliating, it's not just the kid who said it who knows, it's the entire school or class," Dr. Levy-Warren told the *Times*. "In the past, if you made a misstep, it was a limited number of people who would know about it."

True enough. In the old days (before 2004), if you were tormented at school, when the bell rang at three o'clock you could go home to your own neighborhood and have fourteen hours to forget about your difficulties with your peers at school. On weekends you could escape them completely.

Summer vacation could be three months of restorative peace and freedom from the bullies at school. When I was a kid, during those three months I never saw the kids in my class unless they happened to live in my immediate neighborhood. You'd go back to school in September and be amazed at how your friends had changed. Some had grown over the summer, others had gained or lost weight—it was like meeting them all over again.

Today, the typical adolescent is wired to his or her peer group twenty-four hours a day, seven days a week, twelve months a year. No longer is there a judgment-free zone. The social judge and jury are at work relentlessly. The pressure never lets up. Even in wealthy communities, social media can be a powerful negative social determinant.

As Tavernise pointed out, another significant change is that girls are going through puberty at earlier ages. According to *The New Puberty*, a 2014 book that describes the phenomenon, today the average girl gets her first period at age twelve and a half, compared with about age sixteen at the turn of the twentieth century. That means girls are entering adulthood—at least physically—when they are not yet emotionally equipped to deal with grown-up issues, including peer relationships, sex and gender identity, and increased independence from family.

Experts warn that suicide is just one manifestation of a larger universe of emotional dysfunction. For example, a recent study of millions of injuries in American emergency departments found that among kids aged ten to fourteen, rates of self-harm, including cutting, had more than tripled. This behavior is of particular concern, as it often heralds suicidal behavior.

Our Highly Medicated Children

In the same *New York Times* article, Sabrina Tavernise noted that adolescent girls experience depression at twice the rate of boys, a pattern that continues into adulthood. Depression is being diagnosed with greater frequency, and young people are being prescribed more medication than ever before. Dr. Levy-Warren cautioned that researchers are uncertain whether the rise in depression is because it is being clinically identified more than before, or because more people are actually depressed.

Or could it be because when someone feels "depressed," well-meaning physicians are quick to diagnose and then prescribe medication? As reported by Drugwatch.com, a service of The Peterson Firm, from 2005 to 2008, 3.7 percent of Americans ages twelve to seventeen took antidepressants. A greater number of girls took them than boys, with 2.8 percent of males and 4.6 percent of females in the age group taking antidepressants.

But recent research connected some of the most popular antidepressants—selective serotonin reuptake inhibitors (SSRIs)—to an increased risk in suicide in children. SSRIs can be effective in children, but in a few cases they can trigger abnormal behavior, including the desire to self-harm or even commit suicide.

How about attention deficit/hyperactivity disorder? From 2003 to 2013 doctors diagnosed 6.4 million American children ages four to seventeen with ADHD, representing a 41 percent increase over that decade. Children with ADHD are usually treated with stimulants, including Adderall (amphetamine and dextroamphetamine) and Ritalin (methylphenidate). Side effects from the drugs include headaches, sleeping problems, and loss of appetite. Uncommon but nonetheless serious side effects include personality changes and the development of tics.

When taking stimulants, children with a history of heart conditions may have a higher risk of heart attacks, strokes, and even sudden death. Researchers have also identified rare cases of children experiencing hallucinations, including becoming manic, hearing voices, and being increasingly suspicious without reason.

How about antipsychotics, another highly profitable drug category?

The number of antipsychotics prescribed for children has increased drastically in past decades. As Drugwatch.com reported, from 1995 to 2002, prescriptions of antipsychotics to children ages two to eighteen jumped from half a million to 2.5 million. A *USA Today* report of one pharmacy benefits management company found that from 2001 to 2005, the rate of prescriptions given to people under nineteen years old increased 80 percent.

New types of medications called atypical antipsychotics can have significant side effects in children, including sedation, weight gain, and involuntary movements like dystonia and tardive dyskinesia (TD). (People suffering with TD have fast, involuntary muscle movements, while those suffering from dystonia have involuntarily painful and slow muscle contractions.)

As *Scientific American* reported, serious side effects associated with atypical antipsychotics include cardiovascular disease, high cholesterol, diabetes, and weight gain. In a study of 116 youths with early-onset schizophrenia, after taking risperidone for eight weeks, kids gained an average of eight pounds, whereas children taking olanzapine gained an average of thirteen pounds. These results prompted a safety review board to demand an early end to the trial.

Additionally, a 2013 Vanderbilt University study found that children taking antipsychotics were three times more likely to develop type 2 diabetes than others who did not.

Healthline.com reported that a study examining the use of antipsychotic drugs showed that many children received them for conditions without psychosis. According to a study published in the American Medical Association's journal *Psychiatry*, antipsychotic medications, which are often prescribed for the treatment of bipolar disorder and schizophrenia, are often given to children who may only be exhibiting behavioral problems associated with their age. A research team from Columbia University, Yale, and the National Institute of Mental Health found the highest use of antipsychotics, especially among boys, was in response to aggressive and impulsive behaviors, not psychotic symptoms.

The numbers "suggest that much of the antipsychotic treatment of children and younger adolescents targets age-limited behavioral problems," the study states.

Psychiatrists like Dr. Vilma Gabbay, chief of the pediatric mood and anxiety disorders program and associate professor of psychiatry at the Icahn School of Medicine at Mount Sinai in New York City, find this "alarming." She urges that because of the side effects of antipsychotic medication, doctors should look for other options to control minor aggression in children with ADHD or autism, including stimulant drugs, talk therapy, and parent training.

Talk therapy and parent training—now there's a novel idea!

Chapter 8:

Emerging Health Care Models

In the previous chapters we've presented an overview of the current state of the American health care system as it relates to our national inability to "cure" chronic diseases and seemingly dysfunctional behaviors that don't have an obvious mechanistic cause. No one can deny that the existing health care system can work wonders in many specific areas of disease. Thanks to modern medical technology, the child born with a congenital heart defect can have the defect surgically corrected and go on to live a healthy life. Brain tumors that were once fatal can be safely removed. Laser eye surgery restores vision that once would have been lost. Vaccines have eradicated infectious diseases such as smallpox that once were the scourge of humanity.

At the same time, lifestyle diseases are becoming more prevalent, and for the first time in human history are even killing more people than our traditional foe, infectious diseases. The question is, what do we do about it? How can we reverse this deadly tide?

To date, the most common response of the health establishment has been to try to educate people on why "healthier lifestyles" will help them live longer and be more productive. For example, here are some excerpts of a message given by Allianz Insurance to its Australian customers:

"The decisions you make today can have an enormous impact on your future, and this could not be more true when it comes to your health. The lifestyle that you choose to lead can cause certain lifestyle diseases to develop. Despite having choice and control when it comes down to lifestyle factors—such as what we eat, how often we exercise, whether we choose to smoke and the amount of alcohol we drink—lifestyle diseases remain the leading cause of death in Australia, with heart disease being the most prevalent . . .

"Poor diet and sedentary lifestyles are known contributors to child and adult obesity. Here in Australia, most of us will have the freedom and means to make choices about what we eat, how much we eat and how often. Despite this, ninety-four percent of Australians are not eating the recommended amount of fruit or vegetables as part of their daily diet. To make matters worse, sixty-two percent of Australian adults do not meet National Physical Activity Guidelines . . .

"As people become more aware of the dangers of smoking, fewer adults choose to take up this habit. Despite this decline in the number of smokers, existing smokers still need to think about the long-term effects on their health . . .

"Lifestyle diseases are the leading cause of death in Australia. Take note of the detrimental effects unhealthy habits may have on your well-being and future, and minimize your risk of developing a lifestyle disease. You have the power to change your lifestyle, and you also have control over making your family's financial future secure."

You have the power! Despite being well intentioned, it sounds like a lecture, with the message being that if you'd just get off your duff, eat healthier, and quit smoking, you'd live longer and be happier. Objectively, everything in the message is absolutely true. If you did the things Allianz told you to do, you'd improve your health. The problem is that many patients *know* what they need to do and yet repeatedly make compensatory choices that are unhealthy. Why? Are they lazy or not well informed? Or is the reason that there's a powerful hidden force at work that's difficult to resist? Despite our many technological successes and the exhortations of the health care industry that people have the power to improve their health, many serious health issues remain hidden in the shadows. These stubborn health problems are characterized by the existence of a continuum of emotional distress and the emotional dimensions of health care. We see that too many serious diseases and what appear to be dysfunctional behaviors don't respond to an application of medical technology or to the simplistic idea that people just need to be better educated to make healthy choices or have easier access to health care. To break through to the next level of health and longevity, we need a new approach.

Fortunately, caregivers are recognizing the need for new pathways as they struggle to understand why people do not change their behavior in the face of overwhelming evidence. We need to be more effective at motivating people. People want to feel better, and historical medical practices have not balanced the need to feel better emotionally as well as physically. Even the notion of integration in its many forms has often meant integrating medical specialties. What we need is to integrate the biological dimensions with the emotional dimensions of health care. Innovation and transformation are the oft-repeated themes in health care reform today. Three emerging concepts, intended to better motivate, connect with, and improve care, are *patient activation, patient engagement,* and *integrated care.*

Patient Activation

The term "patient activation" refers to the ability and willingness of patients to take action to manage their own health and care. Patient activation is put on an equal footing with understanding one's role in the care process and possessing the confidence, skill, and knowledge to manage one's health and health care.

Activation is not the same thing as compliance, which emphasizes getting patients to follow medical advice.

In their 2013 article in *Health Affairs* entitled "What the Evidence Shows About Patient Activation: Better Health Outcomes and Care Experiences; Fewer Data on Costs," researchers Judith H. Hibbard and Jessica Greene reviewed the available evidence of the contribution that patient activation makes to health outcomes, costs, and patient experience.

They reported on research results connecting patient activation with patient experience, costs, and health outcomes, which over the past decade have grown substantially. In addition to reviewing the strength of those results, the authors pointed to key research gaps and addressed two important policy questions: Can patients who are disengaged and not activated become activated? And what are effective strategies for activating patients?

The authors used the Patient Activation Measure to measure activation of patients with a range of conditions and economic backgrounds. The assessment consists of thirteen items, and patients score between 0 and 100 based on how they respond to questions about their knowledge, confidence, and beliefs, and in how they manage health-related tasks. The score is then used to assign people to one of four levels, ranging from least activated (level 1) to most activated (level 4).

Examples of questions include the following:

"I know what treatments are available for my health problems."

"I am confident that I can tell whether I need to go to the doctor or whether I can take care of a health problem myself."

"I am confident that I can tell a doctor my concerns, even when he or she does not ask."

Responses were degrees of agreement or disagreement.

People who score higher on the Patient Activation Measure are more likely to avoid unhealthy behaviors such as smoking and illegal drug use, and are more likely to engage in healthy behavior such as getting regular exercise and eating a healthy diet. They are more likely to seek preventive behavior such as having regular check-ups, screenings, and immunizations.

Chronically ill patients with higher activation levels are more likely to perform regular self-monitoring at home; obtain regular chronic care, such as foot exams for diabetes; and adhere to their treatment plan.

Patients who are highly activated are more likely to know about treatment guidelines for their condition, prepare questions for a visit to the doctor, and seek out health information, including comparisons of the quality of health care providers.

In contrast, those who are less activated are much more likely to have medical needs that go unmet, and are twice as likely to delay medical care.

The authors concluded that policies and interventions designed to enhance the role of patients in managing their own health care can lead to better outcomes, and that patient activation can—and should—be measured as a vital stepping-stone on the way to improved outcomes.

Patient activation, however, is a two-way street, with the physician on the other end. Note that one of the questions cited above was "I am confident that I can tell a doctor my concerns, even when he or she does not ask."

Consider this story about two patients who were not confident and whose physicians did nothing to build their confidence, as written by Gina Kolata in her 2016 article for *The New York Times* entitled "Why Do Obese Patients Get Worse Care? Many Doctors Don't See Past the Fat."

Patty Nece, age fifty-eight, went to an orthopedist because of an ache in her hip. She had been on a diet and had lost nearly seventy pounds and, although she still had more weight to lose, was feeling optimistic about herself.

That is, until the doctor walked in.

"He came to the door of the exam room, and I started to tell him my symptoms," Nece told the author. "He said: 'Let me cut to the chase. You need to lose weight.'"

She said while the doctor never examined her, he made a curt diagnosis: "You have obesity pain." This is the message he forwarded to her internist.

In fact, she later learned, her hip was aching because she had progressive scoliosis, a condition not caused by obesity.

Another woman—who asked not to be named to protect her privacy—suddenly found it difficult to take the few steps from her bedroom to her kitchen. At age forty-six, the normally routine effort left her gasping for breath. She hurried to a local urgent care center, where after a cursory examination the doctor told her the problem was excess weight pressing on her lungs.

The doctor said she had only one thing wrong with her: she was overweight.

"I started to cry," said the woman. "I said, 'I don't have a sudden weight pressing on my lungs. I'm really scared. I'm not able to breathe.'"

"That's the problem with obesity," she said the doctor told her. "Have you ever considered going on a diet?"

It turned out that the woman's shortness of breath was caused by several small blood clots in her lungs, a life-threatening condition that was unrelated to her weight.

When treating obese patients, doctors may be swayed by baseless assumptions, attributing symptoms like shortness of breath to obesity without investigating other likely causes. One result is that patients become confused and may give up trying to get an accurate diagnosis. Patients who are activated are more likely to closely question their doctor and, if necessary, find other opinions.

Patient Engagement

"Patient engagement" refers to a broader concept that includes a patient's activation as well as the interventions designed to enhance activation, and then the patient's resulting behavior, such as engaging in regular physical exercise or obtaining appropriate preventive care. The focus on activation and engagement rather than compliance stems from the realization that the vast majority of the time patients manage their health on their own, making decisions every day that affect their health and the price they have to pay.

Patient engagement is one strategy to achieve the Triple Aim of:

1. Improved health outcomes.
2. Better patient care.
3. Lower costs.

The background, as described by Julia James in "Health Policy Brief: Patient Engagement," published *in Health Affairs*, February 14, 2013, is that in the United States health care is a complicated subject, and many patients aren't sure how to go about procuring even basic health services and information. Many patients lack what's called "health literacy," which can be defined as a clear understanding of their condition and the treatments that are available, affordable, and accessible. They find that the US health care system is too often indifferent to their desires and needs, and so they either give up or seek refuge in welcoming but risky alternative treatments. Many practitioners either can't or won't provide the information that their patients need to make the best decisions about their own care and treatment. And when patients do receive complete information, the complexity can be overwhelming, pushing patients to be unsure of their choices. People with a low level of health literacy can't always adhere to treatment regimens or follow instructions on how to care for themselves; for example, they may not understand how and when to take their medication.

Recognizing these challenges, the 2001 Institute of Medicine report, *Crossing the Quality Chasm: A New Health System for the 21st Century*, specified reforms with the goal of a "patient-centered" health care system. The problem is that patient-centered approaches, while valuable, will not be truly patient centered if we don't understand what motivates people and the emotional dimensions of health-related behaviors. The report proposed a system that provides care that is "respectful of and responsive to individual patient preferences, needs, and values, and ensuring that patient values guide all clinical decisions." The field of patient engagement has emerged, in part, out of this recognition.

Kristin Carman and her coauthors, of the American Institutes for Research, have proposed a framework that conceptualizes patient engagement taking place on three main levels:

1. Direct patient care, in which patients receive information about a condition and can give their opinions about their preferences for treatment. This form of engagement allows patients and providers to make decisions based on the medical evidence, patients' preferences, and clinical judgment.

2. Organizational design and governance, in which health care organizations get input from both patients and stakeholders to ensure they will be as responsive as possible to patients' needs.

3. Policy making, in which patients and stakeholders are involved in the decisions that society and communities make about laws, policies, and regulations in health care and public health.

Some commentators urge the health care industry and policy makers to be leery of embracing "patient engagement" as the catch phrase of the day. In "What Does 'Patient Engagement' Really Mean?" published in *Healthcare IT News*, Michelle Ronan Noteboom wrote, "To be clear: I fully support engaging patients in their own health to achieve better outcomes. I am just not a big fan of that ill-named term."

She pointed out that patient engagement is used to describe everything from "patient portals to social media strategies, from tracking vitals with wearables to patients actively participating in their own health and wellness. Everyone seems to be talking about patient engagement, even though we can't agree on what it is."

She reported that at a recent Healthcare Information and Management Systems Society (HIMSS) conference, patient engagement was a popular subject, where educational sessions offered suggestions for engaging patients, and exhibitors promoted patient engagement tools. During the event, HIMSS, which is focused on information technology, published a leadership survey revealing that a majority of the respondents identified consumer and patient considerations, including quality of care, satisfaction, and engagement, as the issues of great concern to their organizations in the near future. They also pointed to the IT strategies most often used to actively engage patients in their care. Eighty-two percent of respondents said they engage patients through their organization's website, while 87 percent reported their organizations offer a portal that enables patients to pay bills, access their medical records, and schedule appointments.

As Noteboom noted, IT departments are limited in their ability to create patient engagement, and a weakness of this engagement would be for leaders to view portals and websites not only as a "strategy" for engaging patients, but as the actual solution.

It seems like every industry segment likes to tout its efforts to promote patient engagement. Here's an excerpt from *The Patient Engagement Playbook*, published online by The Office of the National Coordinator for Health Information Technology (ONC), which is located within the Office of the Secretary for the US Department of Health and Human Services (HHS):

"Across the nation, patients' phones and computers are teeming with patient-generated health data: health-related data that patients create, record, or gather to help address a health concern. They include:

- Health history
- Treatment history
- Biometric data, like blood pressure readings
- Symptoms
- Lifestyle choices, like diet and exercise habits

"As the amount of available data has grown, so too has our ability to collect, organize, and make sense of it all. More and more health systems are aggregating patient-generated health data in their EHRs and relying on these data to conduct remote monitoring—that is, to track patients' wellness outside the clinic.

"Providers can take advantage of these patient-generated health data to fill information gaps—and, ultimately, improve clinical decision-making, care delivery, and health outcomes."

Provider websites and patient portals are useful, but an organization that simply has the technology to support the viewing, downloading, and transmitting of medical data doesn't automatically translate to patients participating in their own health and wellness.

Patients need to participate in their own health and wellness because such involvement often leads to better outcomes and lowers costs. Making portals and websites available to patients is a positive first step, but true participation requires dedicated human interaction and the participation of physicians and staff.

When pondering this current fascination with all things digital, one cannot help but think about the story of Dr. Vincent Felitti, who took the time to ask his obese patient, who had been raped a year earlier, about her life and her feelings about herself. While she was outwardly unhappy about her weight, she confided to Dr. Felitti, "Overweight is overlooked, and that's the way I need to be."

This small step toward better health was the result of patient engagement on a personal, one-on-one level. It took both time and trust, and you can't get that from the Internet.

In contrast, we recall the story about Patty Nece, whose orthopedist bluntly informed her that her hip pain was due to her obesity. She later learned that her hip ached because she had progressive scoliosis. She was an "engaged" patient who went to her doctor for help—but her doctor was anything but engaged.

Patient's Bill of Rights

As a reflection of the growing concern with patient activation and engagement, various organizations have developed statements that share the name "Patient's Bill of Rights." The purpose of these statements has been to both empower patients with the sense that they should not be reluctant to assert themselves, as well as serve notice to health care providers about the professional standards they should be meeting. While none of these statements carry the force of law—a Patients' Bill of Rights was considered by the United States Congress in 2001 but didn't pass—they signify an awareness of the complexity and frequent contentiousness of the American health care system.

The US Advisory Commission on Consumer Protection and Quality in the Health Care Industry wrote a Patient's Bill of Rights in

1998. Called "The Consumer Bill of Rights and Responsibilities," it was created to try to reach three major goals:

1. To help patients feel more confident in the US health care system, the Bill of Rights:
   - Assures that the health care system is fair and it works to meet patients' needs.
   - Gives patients a way to address any problems they may have.
   - Encourages patients to take an active role in staying or getting healthy.
2. To stress the importance of a strong relationship between patients and their health care providers.
3. To stress the key role patients play in staying healthy by laying out rights and responsibilities for all patients and health care providers.

The eight key areas of the Patient's Bill of Rights Information for patients are:

1. **Information disclosure:** You have the right to accurate and easily understood information about your health plan, health care professionals, and health care facilities. If you speak another language, have a physical or mental disability, or just don't understand something, help should be given so you can make informed health care decisions.
2. **Choice of providers and plans**: You have the right to choose health care providers who can give you high-quality health care when you need it.

3. **Access to emergency services:** If you have severe pain, an injury, or sudden illness that makes you believe that your health is in danger, you have the right to be screened and stabilized using emergency services. You should be able to use these services whenever and wherever you need them, without needing to wait for authorization and without any financial penalty.

4. **Taking part in treatment decisions:** You have the right to know your treatment options and to take part in decisions about your care. Parents, guardians, family members, or others that you choose can speak for you if you cannot make your own decisions.

5. **Respect and nondiscrimination.** You have a right to considerate, respectful care from your doctors, health plan representatives, and other health care providers that does not discriminate against you.

6. **Confidentiality (privacy) of health information:** You have the right to talk privately with health care providers and to have your health care information protected. You also have the right to read and copy your own medical record. You have the right to ask that your doctor change your record if it is not correct, relevant, or complete.

7. **Complaints and appeals:** You have the right to a fair, fast, and objective review of any complaint you have against your health plan, doctors, hospitals, or other health care personnel. This includes complaints about waiting times, operating hours, the actions of health care personnel, and the adequacy of health care facilities.

8. **8. Consumer responsibilities:** In a health care system that protects consumer or patients' rights, patients should expect to take on some responsibilities to get well and/or stay well (for instance, exercising and not using tobacco). Patients are expected to do things like treat health care workers and other patients with respect, try to pay their medical bills, and follow the rules and benefits of their health plan coverage. Having patients involved in their care increases the chance of the best possible outcomes and helps support a high-quality, cost-conscious health care system.

While all of these ideals are laudable, none of them address the root causes of why Americans are getting sicker; they primarily seek to make the existing health care system function more smoothly.

Integrated Care

In health policy circles, another buzzword *du jour* is "integrated care." It mainly refers to the integration of physical health care and behavioral health care for those with a mental health diagnosis. On an operational level it means shared services or a physical co-location of physical health and mental health services. It's characterized by communication and collaboration among health care professionals. Integrated health care is unique because of information sharing among team members related to patient care as well as the establishment of comprehensive treatment plans to address patients' biological, psychological, and social needs.

While the concept is popular, the nomenclature is uncertain. As discussed in an article published by Essential Hospitals Institute, a subsidiary of America's Essential Hospitals, titled "Integrated Health Care Literature Review," under the umbrella term "integrated care" are more than seventy terms or phrases and 175 concepts or definitions, including the following:

- Accountable care systems
- Clinically integrated systems
- Integrated health organizations
- Integrated delivery networks
- Integrated health services
- Integrated health care delivery
- Organized systems of care
- Organized delivery systems

Definitions of "integrated delivery system" (IDS)—as a hospital trade association, America's Essential Hospitals would naturally be focused on health care delivery—include:

"An organized, coordinated and collaborative network that: (1) links various health care providers, via common ownership or contract, across three domains of integration—economic, noneconomic, and clinical—to provide a coordinated, vertical continuum of services to a particular patient population or community; and (2) is accountable both clinically and fiscally for the clinical outcomes and health status of the population or community served, and has systems in place to manage and improve them."[1]

Another definition is, "An organization which 'uses corporate structure, strategic alliances, governance, management approaches, culture, financial practices, clinical information systems, and other tools to facilitate and ensure delivery of this type of care.'"[2]

A third is, "The management and delivery of health services so that the clients receive a continuum of preventive and curative services, according to their needs over time and across different levels of the health system" (World Health Organization's working definition of IDS).

From the perspective of the health care industry, there are two main types of integration used in integrated delivery systems (IDS): horizontal and vertical.

"Horizontal integration" is defined by the Pan American Health Organization as "the coordination of activities across operating units that are at the same stage in the process of delivering services." Organizations use horizontal integration to group together similar levels of care under one management umbrella. Such groupings allow the organization to consolidate resources through increased efficiency and economies of scale.

Some systems have demonstrated success with horizontal integration by acquiring and merging reputable hospitals and then posting

---

1 "Integrated Delivery Systems: The Cure for Fragmentation," Alain C. Enthoven, PhD, AJMC.com, December 15, 2009, http://www.ajmc.com/journals/supplement/2009/a264_09dec_hlthpolicycvrone/a264_09dec_enthovens284to290.
2 Moore, Keith D. and Dean C. Coddington, "Multiple Paths to Integrated Health Care" *Healthcare Financial Management*, December 2009.

higher reimbursement rates from payers willing to pay a higher price for their services.

"Vertical integration" is defined by the Pan American Health Organization as "the coordination of services among operating units that are at different stages of the process of delivery patient services." Essential Hospitals Institute points to these and many other definitions as evidence of the lack of clarity and agreement about the IDS concept. Indeed, the wealth of position papers and scholarly articles makes you wonder about Patty Nece and her progressive scoliosis, or our friend Roy who feels lousy and who's headed for another heart attack, or Janice, who had diabetes but who can't stop eating cakes and sweets. Amid all the jargon and posturing, what happens to the people who are suffering and who can't find relief no matter how integrated their care might be?

Sweden and Chains of Care

In her 2010 article "What Does It Take to Make Integrated Care Work?" Jenny Grant, writing for McKinsey & Co., tackled the problem of defining what integrated care is—and is not.

She wrote that, too often, providers focus on narrow courses of treatment rather than the patient's overall well-being. In contrast, in an integrated care setting the various stakeholders involved in patient care are brought together so that, from the patient's perspective, the services delivered are seamless and coordinated. By taking an approach that's more comprehensive, integrated care can offer patients more efficient and higher quality care that better meets their needs.

While different approaches have been used to integrate care, they all design each stage of care delivery around what is best for patients.

These varying approaches can be grouped into three broad categories:

Integration between payors and providers. These efforts are designed to more closely coordinate care planning, commissioning, and delivery, and make it easier to ensure that the incentives are designed to encourage providers to enhance quality of care while lowering their costs. For example, for patients who have suffered an acute coronary event, to provide better care Kaiser Permanente has leveraged its integrated functions of payor and provider. It's better able to identify all such patients and offer them coordinated follow-up care. The program has significantly decreased the need for costly emergency interventions and reduced the risk of early and unnecessary death.

Integration between health care and community care. These efforts coordinate a wider range of services, including community nursing services and social services. More than a decade ago, Sweden took the lead in this area. For example, care is taken before a disabled or elderly patient can be discharged from a Swedish hospital to either go home or to a lower-acuity care setting. Before the patient is released, a caseworker from the city social services agency and a health care professional from the hospital work in tandem to create a plan of action ensuring the patient will receive the follow-up services they need. This strategy has allowed Sweden to both reduce the number of patients they keep in the hospital once they're able to be released and improve the care they receive after they leave the hospital. **Integration between primary care and secondary care.** These efforts are designed to ensure more appropriate use of health care resources; to provide a package of services for patients; or to improve care coordination, especially for people requiring long-term care, who, by definition, include elderly and chronically ill patients. Grant noted that Polikum, the largest provider of integrated outpatient health services in Germany, exemplifies this approach. It operates under the philosophy that patients should be able to access a variety of necessary outpatient care services under one roof. At Polikum's clinics in Berlin, patients can consult nutritionists, specialists, primary care physicians, and other health professionals. They can also get blood tests and fill prescriptions. Polikum executives have estimated that during the first year after adopting this strategy, the company's hospitalization costs were reduced by about half.

The Swedish model mentioned by Grant merits further discussion. As Monica Andersson Bäck, PhD and Johan Calltorp, MD noted in their 2015 article "The Norrtälje Model: A Unique Model for Integrated Health and Social Care in Sweden," the Norrtälje model is a Swedish initiative that transformed the funding and organization of health and social care in order to provide better care for older people with complex needs. Named for a locality and the seat of Norrtälje Municipality, Stockholm County, Sweden, with 17,275 inhabitants in 2010, the goal of the model tested in Norrtälje is to promote and develop vertical and horizontal cooperation, with the goal of better responding to the community's needs for integrated health care and social services. The model is characterized by three activities:

1. An increased focus on health promotion for the population.
2. Funding responsibilities for a single population.
3. Creating a common and integrated health and social care organization to deliver enhanced patient and user benefit.

Making a change like the Norrtälje model requires involvement from external expertise and a systematic, strategic plan. It can take time for the broad changes at the macro-organization level to result in microlevel changes in care providing. The integration was hindered by an unwieldy structure that included professional training, status, legal aspects for documentation systems and different traditions, legislation, and working practices, which remained long after the implementation started.

Several facilitating factors contributed to the success of the model, including the local Norrtälje spirit; the possibility of closing the local hospital, which helped engage the community; and the intense management work, shared vision, commitment, and training and concrete integration activities. Although the process was cumbersome and is still evolving, in the end the Norrtälje model altered how care was delivered and improved the quality of care. With no additional tax burden, it was made possible by a community vision and determination to make that vision a reality.

Also in Sweden we see the emerging concept of "chains of care," as discussed by Bengt Åhgren in his article "Chain of Care Development in Sweden: Results of a National Study." Chains of care are designed to be a counterbalance to the growing fragmentation of Swedish health care, with improved quality of care as the most important reason for developing a new approach.

The effort is being made in response to three major driving forces in health care development.

First is the increased specialization in health care. Primarily due to health care personnel acquiring deeper medical knowledge in ever-narrowing areas, this leads to diminished knowledge of closely related specialties. The reality is that improved health care not only requires better professionals but better systems of work.

Second, decentralization has progressed to the extent that Swedish health care could be seen as frontline driven, where frontline managers have significant responsibilities and enough authority to act independently.

Third is the principle of a professional organization. In their treatment of patients, Swedish nurses, physicians, and other providers independently make decisions, and they take personal responsibility for those decisions. In this kind of organizational culture, striving for common health care goals is less important because the emphasis is on the treatment of the immediate problem for which the patient is seeking help.

Individually and together, these three factors have strengthened the autonomous functions of today's health care. Since it's unusual to have one person solely responsible for the full treatment process and decision-making power, difficulties arise in the coordination of activities for patient treatment, particularly if they are to be carried out in several different functions. Since these driving forces tend to fragment a patient's care, the result is a growing interest in integrated care and chains of care in the Swedish health system.

Chains of care are defined as "coordinated activities within health care, linked together to achieve a qualitative final result for the patient. A chain of care often involves several responsible authorities and medical providers." One way of being proactive and preparing the health care system for active consumers would be quickly involving patients in the health care processes that affect them. Research suggests that patients who take an active role in managing their care experience a better health outcome. Committed patients can also be important agents of change within the professional value system and help affect change among health care personnel to improve integration between different health care providers. The next step is to design chains of care that hold patients in high esteem as partners and contributors in treatment procedures, not merely as objects. That is to say, create a system of integrated care not only within the boundaries of the existing health care delivery system, but also with the goal of the complete integration of the patients.

Focusing on the Socioeconomic Determinants of Health

Today we're seeing increased attention to negative social determinants in the current environment of the patient, which is a step in the right direction. As Thomas R. Frieden, MD, MPH proposed in his 2010 article "A Framework for Public Health Action: The Health Impact Pyramid," published in the *American Journal of Public Health*, our health care dollars and resources could be allocated according to percentages resembling a pyramid with five tiers.

From the broad base to the narrow top, the five tiers are:

Tier 1. Efforts to address socioeconomic determinants of health. At the broad base of the pyramid, indicating interventions with the greatest potential impact, this tier of the health impact pyramid represents poverty reduction and improved education that help form the basic foundation of a society. In high-poverty areas, significant improvements in health will require improved economic opportunities and strengthened infrastructure, including reliable transportation, sanitation, electricity, and other basic services.

Tier 2. Change the context to make individuals' default decisions healthy. "Default decisions" are those in which the individual has no real choice. For example, many scientists believe that fluoridated water, which simply comes out of your tap, not only improves dental health but brings economic benefits by reducing productivity losses and health spending.

Tier 3. Clinical interventions that require limited contact but confer long-term protection. A good example is colonoscopy, which can significantly reduce colon cancer and for most people is only needed once every five to ten years. Another example is immunization, which scientists say prevents 2.5 million deaths per year among children around the world.

Tier 4. Ongoing direct clinical care. Interventions to prevent cardiovascular disease can have a significant impact on the public health of a society; and while comprehensive clinical care can make people healthier and live longer, these interventions are too often limited by imperfect effectiveness, erratic and unpredictable adherence, and lack of patient access to the appropriate care.

Tier 5. Health education and counseling. The author considers this to be the least effective, and therefore the smallest, part of the pyramid. As we have seen so often in this book, simply urging people to adopt "healthy habits" and to "lose the excess weight" is like putting a coat of paint on a building whose foundation is crumbling. For example, efforts to correct our obesogenic environment include exhortations to improve diet and increase physical activity, which for many people, especially those with untreated ACEs, have little or no effect. Both in the United States and globally, obesity rates are rising, and the author reports that two thirds of these individuals have been counseled by a health care provider to lose weight, yet our collective intake of calories and fat continues to rise.

The author says that interventions focusing on the lower and more broad levels of the pyramid tend to be more effective because they reach wider segments of society and require less individual effort.

At the top tiers, interventions are designed to help individuals rather than entire populations. In reality, the pyramid's higher levels achieve only a limited level of public health impact by even the best programs; this is due to their dependence on long-term individual behavior change. As Geoffrey Rose wrote in *Rose's Strategy of Preventive Medicine*, "Personal life-style is socially conditioned . . . Individuals are unlikely to eat very differently from the rest of their families and social circle . . . It makes little sense to expect individuals to behave differently than their peers; it is more appropriate to seek a general change in behavioral norms and in the circumstances which facilitate their adoption."

While it's a good framework, the five-tiered pyramid unfortunately does not seek to uncover and treat *why* people make unhealthy choices. It overlooks the emotional dimension of health care, which we have seen can be critically important to recognize and treat.

The Positive Effects of a Doctor's Bedside Manner

We increasingly are hearing the idea that the physician needs to be cognizant of his or her behavior toward the patient. This idea is as old as the ancient Greeks, who were specific about the bedside manners of physicians. Included in the Hippocratic Corpus is this comment:

"The physician ought also to be confidential, very chaste, sober, not a winebibber, and he ought to be fastidious in everything, for this is what the profession demands. He ought to have an appearance and approach that is distinguished. Everything ought to be in moderation, for these things are advantageous, so it is said. Be solicitous in your approach to the patient, not with head thrown back (arrogantly) or hesitantly with lowered glance, but with head inclined slightly as the art demands.

"He ought to hold his head humbly and evenly; his hair should not be too much smoothed down, nor his beard curled like that of a degenerate youth. Gravity signifies breadth of experience. He should approach the patient with moderate steps, not noisily, gazing calmly at the sick bed. He should endure peacefully the insults of the patients since those suffering from melancholic or frenetic ailments are likely to hurl evil words at physicians."

As reported in the article "Physicians' Bedside Manner Affects Patients' Health," published in *The Advisory Board Daily Briefing*, a recent review of clinical trials reinforced the idea that a doctor's bedside manner can greatly impact patients' health, aiding their efforts to lose weight, lower their blood pressure, or manage painful symptoms.

The review found that with respect to the specific health outcomes in patients with asthma, diabetes, obesity, or osteoarthritis, relationship-focused training had a measurable positive effect. Among other things, such training—and the resulting bedside approach—could affect weight loss, pain levels, blood sugar, blood pressure, and lipid levels.

Here's the most startling finding: researchers reported that for preventing heart attack, a doctor's bedside manner exceeded the reported effects of both cholesterol-lowering statins and low-dose aspirin.

More effective than prescribed statins? Don't tell the pharmaceutical industry. By 2019, revenues for the cholesterol-lowering drugs market are expected to reach nearly twenty-five billion dollars.

"Our results show that the beneficial effects of a good patient-clinician relationship on health care outcomes are of similar magnitude to many well-established medical treatments," said lead author John Kelley, a psychologist at Massachusetts General Hospital. He added, "Many of these medical treatments, while very important, need to balance their benefits against accompanying unwanted side effects. In contrast, there are no negative side effects to a good patient-clinician relationship."

The review did not discover which interventions provided the most benefit, noted Alan Christensen, a professor of psychology at the University of Iowa who was not involved in the study. He added that patients differ in what characteristics make a "good" doctor, including how much information they want shared, their views on self-management, and how open they are to personal questions.

As Barry D. Silverman, MD noted his article "Physician Behavior and Bedside Manners: The Influence of William Osler and The Johns Hopkins School of Medicine," it's a good idea to distinguish between the art and practice of medicine. As we develop better techniques for diagnosis, improved therapies for treatment, and new technologies, the *practice* of medicine changes with time. But because human nature is unchanging, the *art* of medicine remains constant over the millennia. As they have since ancient times, when patients come to the exam room they bring their fear, anxiety, and self-pity with them. The doctor has always had the responsibility to provide hope and calm their fears. The successful doctor has a bedside manner that is supportive, empathetic, compassionate, and humane. He does not, as Patty Nece experienced, brusquely dismiss his patient with the admonition that she needs to lose weight—and without even examining her.

As Dr. Atul Gawande, a surgeon at the Brigham and Women's Hospital in Boston and an assistant professor at the Harvard School of Public Health, wrote in his book *Better: A Surgeon's Notes on Performance,*

"It is unsettling how little it takes to defeat success in medicine. You come as a professional equipped with expertise and technology. You do not imagine that a mere matter of etiquette could foil you. But the social dimension turns out to be as essential as the scientific matter of how casual you should be, how formal, how reticent, how forthright. Also how apologetic, how self-confident, how money minded. In this work against sickness, we begin not with genetic or cellular interactions but with human ones."

These tools are good for everyone. They help build health in all people, and restore health in those with traumatic stress.

Chapter 9:

Health Care Policy: Changing the Underlying Assumptions

Action to advance the emotional dimensions of health is not placed solely at the feet of health care practitioners. We have discussed the impact of social, economic, and cultural sources on traumatic experiences, toxic stress, and chronic disease. The performance of the United States in all domestic policy arenas is a factor in our high expenditures and low results noted by the Commonwealth fund. Governments should not only see but act to eradicate the cost, in both human and financial terms, of inadequate access to housing, lack of safety, and abuse in all its forms. This book at its very essence is a policy bridge between medicine and the social determinants of health.

It is within medicine's scope to acknowledge the deleterious effects of traumatic experiences and toxic stress on people's health. Medicine is in a unique position to help people understand the role of their current compensatory behaviors in maintaining their emotional balance and functioning (which is a good thing) while on the other hand dramatically contributing to chronic disease (a bad thing). We need to change our health care system to be more responsive to patients who

189

come through the door with chronic diseases that seem intractable and must be addressed in the context of ACEs and toxic stress.

Making all these changes will not be quick or easy. What we need is a pivot in our approach to health care that is reminiscent of a similar pivot that occurred over one hundred years ago: the innovative campaign against cholera in London in the nineteenth century.

It's a fascinating story that we briefly mentioned in the introduction.

On August 31, 1854, after several outbreaks had occurred elsewhere in the city, a major outbreak of cholera reached the London neighborhood of Soho. Cholera is a particularly nasty disease. With horrible symptoms of vomiting, diarrhea, and violent cramps, it causes dehydration so severe and rapid the blood thickens in the veins and the skin becomes blue and corpse-like. Cholera victims can die in a matter of hours after the disease takes hold.

Over the first three days of the Soho outbreak, 127 people on or near Broad Street died. During the next week, three quarters of the residents had fled the area. By September 10, five hundred people had died and some parts of the city had a mortality rate as high as 12.8 percent. By the end of the outbreak, 616 people had died.

For much of the century, most European and American physicians had believed cholera was a locally produced miasmatic disease—a term derived from the ancient Greek that means "pollution" or "bad air." There was a moral component as well; it was a common assumption that people of low moral fiber or who had uncivilized personal practices were more likely to get cholera when they were exposed to these miasmas and environmental conditions. In a sense this was true, but only because wealthy people were more likely to have access to clean water, not because they were of higher moral character. The fact that wealthy folk became sick at a lower rate was used as a moral bludgeon against those who lived in harm's way through no fault of their own.

No effective treatment for cholera was available at the time. Patients with families received care at home. Physicians, when called, would use unscientific treatments, including bleeding or opium, which were all they had and represented the current "standard of care." Homeopathic methods were popular among the middle and upper classes, but none were successful.

John Snow, a London physician, scientifically investigated the pattern of the outbreak. As the result of his research, Snow created a map with dots to illustrate how cases of cholera were clustered around a public water pump located in Soho at the intersection of Broad Street and Cambridge Street.

On September 8, city officials agreed to disable the pump by removing its handle. The outbreak, which may have already been waning, quickly subsided.

Why this particular pump? They didn't know it at the time—the action of bacterial infection was still undiscovered—but bacteria from human fecal matter was the cause of the disease. Despite not knowing the actual cause, Snow correctly concluded that cholera was transported by contaminated water. It was common at the time for most homes to have a cesspit dug underneath. Years after the outbreak, officials discovered that the Broad Street public well had been dug only three feet from an old cesspit that had begun to leak fecal bacteria. But where did the cholera bacteria come from? They discovered that one cholera-infected baby's nappies—diapers to Americans—had been washed into this cesspit that opened under a nearby house.

Snow's innovative work set an important precedent for epidemiology. His discovery eventually came to influence public health policy and the construction of improved sanitation facilities and sewers. Later, the term "focus of infection" would be used to describe places like the Broad Street pump in which conditions are optimum for transmission of an infection.

Cholera can be controlled by measures that are relatively simple but require a focus on solving the right problem. Risk factors for the disease include poor sanitation, not enough clean drinking water, and poverty. Prevention, which involves improved sanitation and access to clean water, is a far more effective approach than attempting to treat individual cases. If you take a case-by-case approach and try to cure the patients when they get sick, you'll never contain the disease. As we have discussed in this book, the root of the problem for many people with chronic disease is the "why" in their behavior.

When the pivot happened from interventional medicine for the symptoms, to attacking the source of the disease through public health measures, cholera prevention became real. We need to drive a similar pivot with the emotional dimensions of chronic disease.

Changing Our Assumptions

There are always assumptions—sometimes disguised as beliefs—that guide medical practice and decision making. In cholera's heyday, "bad air" was assumed to be the cause, with certain personal behaviors making one more prone to the disease. Doctors treated patients' symptoms as best they could and often prescribed fresh air. Until the assumptions changed, the interventional strategies remained the same.

We have more recent examples of the same assumption-driven missteps as well. As figure 1 outlines, we have made certain assumptions about the causes of chronic disease escalation and the persistence of health care disparities. These assumptions have resulted in a series of interventional strategies, all of which have had at best quite modest, if any, meaningful effect. What do they lack and why do they fail? They do not incorporate the emotional dimensions of health.

Fig 1:

ASSUMPTION	People do not know what to do to be healthy; people need help establishing healthy routines.	People overuse health care because it is free/cheap.	Health disparities due to poor access to primary care; lack of cultural competence.
INTERVENTION	• Health coaches; • Social media–based reminders; • Broad education campaigns.	• Copays. • Cost sharing; • Managed care tools: • Preauthorization; • Expenditure caps; • Utilization review	• Incentives to establish health clinics in distressed neighborhoods; • Increasing numbers of physician's representative of the community being served.
RESULTS	Rates of chronic disease continue to rise; Intractable presentations resulting in growing costs	Delays in care due to personal cost, leading to increased disease burden and cost	Health disparities continue; Health inequity leading to increased disease burden and cost

This book then offers a new assumption from which to develop a series of interventional strategies. This assumption has been long overlooked, yet as we have seen, is undeniable. We all live somewhere along a continuum of emotional distress and do our best to manage life with those constraints. For some, the burden is low. For most of us, some sort of effort to ameliorate the distress is natural and healthy. Until it is not.

Policy and Payors

The overwhelming weight of evidence showing the connection between emotional dimensions of health care and chronic disease should be a call-to-arms for the public health community. Particularly important is that we change our cultural beliefs related to stress, traumatic experiences, and compensatory behaviors. Persistent and widespread myths have spread the belief that many compensatory behaviors are character flaws or signs of weakness. Given this mythology, the reticence on the part of so many to discuss these issues with their physician is both understandable and catastrophic. Public education around the pervasiveness of toxic experiences and the stress they cause, which makes us sick, is critical. Public health education efforts such as smoking cessation, hand washing, and vaccinations are all wonderful examples of how to help people make better choices for themselves or their children.

Once the public is better informed about these issues, physicians will need the capacity to respond. In the historical fee-for-service health care financing where an average pediatric visit is eight minutes, it's extremely difficult to have meaningful conversations on the emotional dimensions of health care. As hospitals are being held more accountable for admissions and readmissions, and individual physicians begin to be paid for value (outcomes), the emotional dimensions of health care will play a critical role in patient engagement and patient activation strategies. Just like the individuals they insure, public and private payors will need to recognize the importance of these kinds of interventions and compensate providers accordingly. Medical school curriculum and CME programs will need to incorporate the emotional dimensions of health care and prepare the next generation of medical professionals for far more effective and comprehensive care.

Social workers and allied health professionals will need to think about becoming supportive adjuncts to medical practitioners to better identify compensatory behaviors, improve strategies for coping, and thus improve health outcomes. Professional associations should begin to identify and promote tools, evidence-based practices, and pathways for team interventions that we know will lead to successful outcomes. At the end of the day, this is what integrated care should truly look like.

Much has been written of late around the notion of disruptive innovation and its role in improving health care, particularly in the area of health technology. Technology innovation is both essential and insufficient—essential in its role to transitioning surgery to something that can be done safely through small arthroscopic tools and in sharing medical records instantly for emergency care. Without simultaneous and equally disruptive innovation in the human side of medicine, aka the emotional dimensions of health, results for patients will continue to be poor.

Signs of Hope for Community Action and Policy

Throughout the book we have reflected on the ideas that the emotional dimensions of health are based on the notion that there is a continuum of emotional distress and that most of us fall somewhere along this continuum. In this section of the prescription, I want to share some encouraging signs of hope. As you read them, you will see grounding in science in both identification of the problem and a solution path. This is to be celebrated. You will also note that these interventions are occurring far out along on the emotional continuum.

For young people living in high-crime areas such as Chicago's South Side, negative social determinants are abundant, and often come in the form of gun violence and death. As Steven Ross Johnson wrote in his article "Gun Violence Survivors and Witnesses Could Face Lifetime of Trauma and Bad Health," published in *Modern Health Care* in 2016, while policy makers struggle to find ways to address America's gun violence problem, another related crisis is slowly growing.

Especially among children, the emotional trauma surrounding exposure to gun violence is undisputed. In 1995, the Centers of Disease Control and Prevention reported that children who had four or more adverse childhood experiences, including experiencing or witnessing a shooting or other violent act, were more likely to engage in either dangerous or self-medicating activities like drinking, smoking, abusing drugs, and engaging in unsafe sex. Those behaviors often lead to chronic health conditions, including diabetes, liver disease, stroke, heart disease, cancer, and sexually transmitted diseases.

A young person's lifespan is adversely affected when they've faced six or more adverse childhood experiences. Such people can expect to live, on average, twenty years shorter than children who have not been exposed to vivid or repeated violence.

"If you grow up in a world where you're not feeling safe, then you feel as though you're under attack whether or not you actually are," said Dr. David Soglin, chief medical officer at La Rabida Children's Hospital, an acute-care pediatric center on Chicago's South Side that specializes in treating children who have been victims of abuse and trauma. "For some kids in our communities, they really *are* under attack."

The challenge is that health care providers don't often consider a patient's exposure to violence as a factor in their overall health or their risk for developing chronic conditions. Many health care providers don't yet recognize the role that the stress of living in communities with high rates of poverty and violence can play in causing poorer health outcomes.

The good news is that we're seeing signs of progress on the horizon.

One of the experts addressing the issue is Charles Ransford, senior director of science and policy with Cure Violence, based at the University of Illinois at Chicago School of Public Health. His organization, originally known as CeaseFire, started in 2000 in the Chicago neighborhood of West Garfield Park, an area characterized by a high rate of homicide.

Cure Violence takes the approach of treating violence as an infectious disease not unlike the cholera epidemic in nineteenth-century

London. They attempt to influence the community to recognize that violence is a poor choice, see there are other solutions to conflict, and ultimately change behavior. "Just as we have now discovered that it is more effective and cost saving to treat drug addiction as a health issue than to punish it," says the organization's mission statement, "it likewise makes more sense to prevent events, provide treatment for people at high risk, and change social norms. Like all potentially harmful behaviors—drug addiction, smoking, eating too much, exercising too little, risky sexual behavior and other behaviors—violent behavior can be understood, diagnosed, and treated through a health lens."

Since 1992, Sinai Health System on Chicago's West Side has offered its "Under the Rainbow" program, an inpatient pediatric ecology program that began by focusing on comprehensive forensic assessments of children and adolescents who were referred for child abuse and/or neglect. Now an outpatient therapy program for children, adolescents, and their families, UTC provides direct services by psychologists, social workers, child development specialists, psychiatrists, and psychology externs. UTR evaluates and treats most psychological disorders of children and adolescents and provides outpatient mental health services for children from birth to age eighteen. UTR has historically specialized in the treatment of the emotional effects of abuse and neglect. Services are also provided for the adult caretakers of these children who are dealing with issues related to those of the child.

"I think we're moving in the right direction," said Dr. Mirna Ballestas, a clinical psychologist who has worked for the past eight years as UTC's program manager. She pointed to the benefit from federal Medicare and Medicaid programs that offer incentives to providers working to prevent diabetes and address negative social determinants such as violence and poverty and violence.

Physicians and Sensitivity to Emotional Trauma

Throughout this book we've seen examples of physicians—well trained and often well meaning—who approach their patients without an understanding or appreciation of the underlying emotional distress that may be a component of their immediate physical complaint.

Efforts are being made to address this problem.

The Trauma Informed Care Project (TIC) of Orchard Place/Child Guidance Center, funded by a grant from the Iowa Department of Human Services, is "an organizational structure and treatment framework that involves understanding, recognizing, and responding to the effects of all types of trauma. It emphasizes physical, psychological and emotional safety for both consumers and providers, and helps survivors rebuild a sense of control and empowerment."

The goal of the Trauma Informed Care Project is twofold:

First, the TIC seeks to educate health care providers about the impact of trauma on both the system and the family. The focus is on examining practices, policies, and organizational structures with the goal of preventing retraumatization of patients by the staff and the health care system at large.

The TIC's second goal is to educate and train health care providers in "evidenced-based trauma-informed services" so that individuals, the community, and the health care system can have the ability to send trauma survivors to receive the appropriate services. It is their goal to present an annual conference, bringing national speakers on trauma to Central Iowa for the annual Psychological Trauma & Juvenile Justices Conference. The project has provided training for therapists, educators, and foster families that has been directed more specifically to their piece of the system and how to enhance services.

The Resilience Project

To more effectively identify and care for children and adolescents who have been exposed to violence, the American Academy of Pediatrics, supported by funding from the Department of Justice, developed resources for medical home teams and pediatricians. The Resilience Project Website provides medical home teams and pediatricians with resources and information that can be used to modify health care processes to better identify, treat, and refer children and young adults who have been exposed to or victimized by violence. The project believes that while exposure to violence is traumatic, the effects need not be permanent, and with proper care and support of their medical home and the community around them, children and young adults can become healthy and thrive.

The Resilience Project was launched in response to reports such as the landmark Adverse Childhood Events (ACE) study and a growing quantity of data, including the report released by the 2008 National Survey of Children's Exposure to Violence that indicated 60 percent of the children surveyed had been exposed to violence—directly or indirectly—in the previous year. Almost half (43%) of the children had experienced an assault. As the AAP stated, *"The effects of this violence could be seen not only in the present moment, but often for many years to come."* Substance use issues, mental health issues, and health problems are just some of the common problems seen in older children and adults affected by violence.

The project advocates that physicians create a trauma-informed practice, which is defined as an organizational structure and treatment framework that involves understanding, recognizing, and responding to the effects of all types of trauma. A trauma-informed practice also emphasizes physical, psychological, and emotional safety for both patients and providers, and helps survivors rebuild a sense of control and empowerment.

It has developed a set of tools that can help provide additional support for the pediatric medical home to identify and more effectively care for children and adolescents who have been exposed to violence. The tools include the ACEs family health history and health appraisal questionnaire, an ACEs screening tool for children and adolescents, a parental ACEs screening tool, a proprietary Resilience Questionnaire, a parental screening questionnaire called "A Safe Environment for Every Kid," and more.

Chapter 10:

The Prescription for Better Health

The United States has hit a wall. We are the biggest spender on health care, witness to incredible advances in medicine, and yet we have a shorter life expectancy and experience more chronic disease than our peers. The compilation of science, art, and experience of emotional dimensions of health, when looked at *in toto*, is the missing piece in the health care value-based equation

Stress has three impacts on people—positive, tolerable, and toxic. Prolonged activation of stress response systems disrupts the development of brain architecture and other organ systems. The extensive research presented shows how prolonged or excessive activation of the stress response system and/or Adverse Childhood Experiences (ACEs) can have damaging effects on behavior, health, and learning for one's entire life.

Incorporating the emotional dimensions of health into health care practice improves health outcomes and starts with the "why" in people's behavior. Compensatory behaviors are a powerful force working beneath the surface that drives people to make choices that, to a detached observer, seem to be irrational. Compensatory behaviors work in the short term, serving a purpose in the life of the individual. Unfortunately, all compensatory behaviors are not created equal. The most familiar and easy-to-access tools—food, alcohol, drugs, excessive care seeking, and social withdrawal—have profound long-term health impacts. Health promotion advocates and doctors profess that changing our "bad" habits will make us *feel better*. It's important to clarify that while a successfully removed "bad" habit will likely make the patient healthier, the loss of a functioning compensatory behavior will make them *feel worse* at a level that will quickly draw them back to the habit for relief. Simplistically trying to remove the "bad" habit that serves a purpose in the individual's life—the compensatory behavior—is a program destined to fail.

Solution pathways must respect the science presented in this book on ACEs, chronic stress, clinical impact, and methods for establishing new behaviors or substitutes. When health practitioners view self-guided attempts to regain allostasis as courageous and important, it opens channels for conversation progression to potential health impact and, if needed, replacement with alternative supports. Fundamental to understanding the emotional dimensions of health care is seeing, valuing, and acting on the "why" behind patients' choices that are leading to disease and/or early death.

Using current models, we view hypertension as a body system malfunction, prescribing a statin medication and providing counseling about diet changes. With an emotional-dimensions-of-health approach, we would view the body responding in the way it should to the chronic fight-or-flight circumstance in which it finds itself.

Assessments expand beyond obtaining blood pressure readings and lab values to include the emotional dimensions of the individual's health. In this example, we may identify a significant ACE score or chronic stress in both a patient's job and family life that have led the patient to become socially withdrawn, angry, and prone to binge drink on the weekends. Addressing this complex scaffolding of emotional triggers and responses is essential to effective treatment outcomes *and* continued life functioning for the patient. Health outcomes will not improve for patients if the prescription for their high blood pressure is a statin and advice that they quit their job or stop caring for their elderly parent.

Within each practice, you will encounter a continuum of distress. Practice along this continuum takes many forms and approaches. On the preventive end, a pediatrician would include a social emotional growth chart in regular check-ups similar to the height/weight chart each parent gets currently. A shared point of reference between primary care practitioners, schools, and families is essential to the achievement of social and emotional developmental milestones. School health and counseling staff can be consistent and intentional in building community through social emotional skill development, anti-bullying programs, and intergenerational programs. Health curriculum can emphasize the pervasiveness of problematic stress and its impact on chronic disease. Helping students to identify stressors in their lives, they can learn effective healthy coping and problem solving skills. These early and preventive strategies seek to ensure that all children are inoculated to stressors as they are to mumps or measles. An example of adult primary care early identification would include a structured conversation on stress levels, leading to a discussion of strategies to get eight hours of sleep, reduce sodium in their diet, and seek out child care supports.

As we move up the interventional intensity toward emerging or moderate stress and traumatic experiences, we need to set new practice norms, which are inclusive of substantive assessment of stress, ACEs, and compensatory behaviors. While exact numbers are not available to quantify this cohort, its significance is captured in the Millbank Memorial Fund primary care study, which noted that 70 percent of all visits to primary care stem from "psychosocial issues," and when symptoms and trauma-related behaviors are left unaddressed, these individuals experience lower productivity, failed relationships, significant distress and dysfunction, and difficulty in caring for children. The salient last finding—when traumatic events and/or toxic stress are not addressed, people cannot care for themselves in health-promoting ways. Our emotional dimensions are as fundamental to our health and well-being as our blood sugar levels or heart rate. As part of every primary care history, health care personnel would administer an ACEs Survey and rigorously research measures of the impact of stress. These tools help inform the health care practitioner of the amount of emotional stress triggering the ill-ness/disease or the stress that is impacting everyday living as a result of the illness/disease. In the context of a doctor/patient relationship, physicians should have conversations with patients about their coping strategies. Are they working? Are they healthy in the long term?

What else might they try? On the low end of these, are they healthy? Primary care practitioners need exemplars and training to make interacting with patients about the role of emotional distress and building positive compensatory behaviors as easy as identifying the need for physical therapy, nutritional counseling, or home health care. There are solutions available, once the topic is broached between patient and practitioner. The practitioner can offer a generic prescription of going for a walk, taking a few minutes out for oneself, or learning meditation using an app like Headspace.

For people who have more significant needs, the conversation should shift to acknowledging the impact of stress on the patient, their noble attempts to cope with it, and alternative options available to strengthen health. These include cognitive reframing, meditation, social connectedness, distress tolerance, emotional self-regulation, yoga, and self-exploration of health-promoting activities. In many situations, the primary care practice can support their patient through the full cycle of identification and new skill acquisition. New partnerships between medical practitioners and alternative health/social/ behavioral health practitioners could also advance the delivery health care inclusive of emotional dimensions.

For those who have suffered with severe emotional trauma, with significant ACE scores and likely comorbid chronic health problems, a more sophisticated integration of care between medical and behavioral health may be needed to ameliorate the profound influences of traumatic experiences. This might well mean professional intervention to reduce or stop abusing substances, short- or long-term use of psychiatric medication, and the assistance of professionally trained therapists to help people through evidenced-based therapeutic approaches such as Trauma-Focused Cognitive Behavioral Therapy and Dialectical Behavioral Therapy.

As we set out to change practice, we must recognize this is not a simple fix. Rational choices for good health are often ignored. Transforming a human life is a very difficult task, and it doesn't always go as intended. The road to health and well-being is long and hard. It is not easy to reverse the effects of years of adversity. If your patients live in a high-crime neighborhood, they cannot just load up the car and move to the suburbs. If your patient is obese, it's extremely difficult to "just eat less." If your patient was routinely beaten as a child, the searing memory can't be erased the way you delete a file on your computer. If you work with Veterans whose fight-or-flight response is at its maximum because of serving in combat in Iraq, they cannot just shut off the hormones when they board the plane to return home. As we've seen in this book, we have to identify the emotional dimensions, understand the "hard-wiring" impacts and introduce integrated physical and emotional health solutions. There are methods to give patients a better chance at good health and a good future.

The Emotional Dimensions of Chronic Conditions

While this book has discussed the emotional component of health, the latest research recognizes that chronic illnesses can themselves produce negative emotional states such as depression, and that such states, which consequently require treatment of their own, can exacerbate the original condition. As Jane Turner and Brian Kelly discussed in their 2000 article entitled "Emotional Dimensions of Chronic Disease," published in the *Western Journal of Medicine*, the emotional dimensions of chronic conditions are often overlooked when medical care is considered. While doctors may be prepared for the biomedical aspects of care, too often they aren't prepared to deal with the challenges of understanding the cultural, social, and psychological dimensions of health and illness.

As any doctor will tell you, patients with chronic conditions often face significant changes to their lifestyle, aspirations, and employment. While many feel sad or depressed about their condition, the feeling is temporary and they soon adjust and look forward to getting better. We all know people who have suffered severe illness or injury and who seem to be unshakably buoyant and optimistic; but sadly, too many others experience prolonged emotional pain and may develop psychiatric disorders, most commonly depression or anxiety. This is the emotional aspect of health and recovery.

To give the problem a numerical context, the authors note that a study of general medical admissions—a broad sampling of people— found that 13 percent of men and 17 percent of women had an affective disorder. Meanwhile, in a more focused sample of patients with conditions such as rheumatoid arthritis or diabetes, those who had an affective disorder was much higher—between 20 and 25 percent. And among patients with cancer and those admitted to the hospital for acute care, rates can exceed 30 percent. We can compare this rate to the prevalence of depression in the general community of 4 to 8 percent.

The emergence of new symptoms in a patient who had appeared to be stable may suggest the patient suffers from emotional distress. The exacerbation of an established illness may indicate complex social or relationship problems, depression, or adjustment difficulties.

The distinction between an adjustment reaction and a depressive illness is often not clear. The diagnosis clarified by examining the patient's risk factors for depression may include a lack of emotional support as well as other negative social determinants such as financial strain or unemployment. The elderly population demonstrates clear ties between depression, disability, and physical illness, and a higher rate of consumption of hospital and medical outpatient services.

Turner and Kelly note that despite diagnostic challenges, diagnosing and treating depression in patients with chronic conditions needs to be a priority. One hurdle is the fact that a person's motivation to gain access to medical care and to follow treatment plans may be impeded by even mild depression. The patient's ability to cope with pain is undermined by depression and hopelessness, which may also damage family relationships.

Among people with a medical illness, the development of depression has been associated with substantial increases in disability and other adverse physical outcomes. Patients who have a cerebrovascular accident and then subsequent depression are more likely to recover significantly less in their ability to perform tasks of daily living, and they tend to die earlier.

Depression also influences heart disease, and among depressed patients, 90 percent of research studies have found elevated rates of mortality from cardiovascular disease. And although the patient with an incurable medical illness who commits suicide may seem at first glance to have acted rationally, most of the patients who commit suicide are also suffering from a depressive illness. Once diagnosed, the question remains of how to treat an underlying emotional disorder.

Turner and Kelly assert that for patients with chronic conditions, the most effective treatment includes a combination of supportive and cognitive psychotherapies that recognize feelings of grief and loss are outcomes of the disease process.

Increasingly, routine medical care is adopting psychosocial interventions, and these approaches seem to be effective. For example, in patients with rheumatoid arthritis, significant improvement on measures of pain, coping, dependency, and helplessness has been achieved with the use of interventions to manage stress.

To better prepare health care providers to understand the emotional components of health, medical education must include the emotional aspects of diseases and their impact on the patient, the patient's family, and the clinicians treating them.

Getting to the Emotional Dimensions Requires Trust and Talking—For Both Health Care Practitioner and Patient

While perhaps a matter of common sense, we must acknowledge and overcome reluctance to engage in conversations about our lives, supports, stressors, and experiences as both practitioners and patients. I am both humbled and reminded of the importance of asking, "What happened to you"—that simple question Dr. Vincent Felitti asked a woman presenting with obesity. His question led to the discovery of childhood sexual abuse and effective long-term treatment. This serendipity led to the ACEs body of work, which has dramatically reduced suffering and improved the health of countless people. The questions are important and lifesaving in helping us to assess, understand, and incorporate the stress—compensatory behavior—pathology—pathway leading to demonstrable positive health outcomes where the patient knows the treatment recommendations are in their best interest and achievable.

Establishing this trust and continuity in relationship is more of a challenge in today's health care world. How we access primary care has changed dramatically. We are more likely to have multiple primary care providers over the course of our lives, due to greater society mobility and changes in provider panels supported by health plans. The nearly exclusive focus on the science part of their interaction, lab values, and symptom reduction and health economics pressing professionals to see a high volume of patients has contributed to both a public perception of disinterest on the part of their health care practitioner and in a perception by practitioners that they do not have time to build trust or ask "difficult questions."

The relationship and trust built into a patient's connection with their primary care practitioner gives primary care the unique opportunity to identify emotional drivers, threats, and compensatory behaviors, and then—perhaps most importantly—to incorporate interventional strategies to improve the patient's health.

As Joseph J. Gallo, MD, PhD wrote in "Emotions and Medicine: What Do Patients Expect from Their Physicians?" published in 1997 in the *Journal of General Internal Medicine*, according to the Global Burden of Disease Report, published at the time by the World Health Organization, depression is the fourth leading cause of disability in the world. It has been projected that by the year 2020, depression will be second only to heart disease. Because many people with depression see a general physician, the primary care setting is key in determining the optimal treatment for depression and other forms of emotional distress.

Surveys have suggested that most patients, and especially patients with functional impairment and emotional distress, believe that emotional distress is within the purview of their physician. What's more, most patients trust that the physician can and will provide counseling, not simply a prescription or a referral to a specialist. The implication is that the average patient would be open to his or her physician's inquiry about potential emotional distress and subsequent counseling about how to manage it.

As for the need for psychiatric care, many patients in the survey who wanted the physician to help them with emotional distress met neither the standard criteria for major depression nor the relaxed set of criteria for "minor" depression. This calls attention to a fundamental question—if a patient comes to their health care provider because of mental or emotional distress but they don't meet standard criteria, then how is a psychiatric disorder to be defined in primary care?

Gallo suggested that perhaps a new classification system is needed when primary care providers encounter mental distress. Such a classification system would acknowledge the patient's own opinion of his or her ability to function, which should be considered when the health care provider formulates the therapeutic plan. In fact, managing mental disorders in primary care may call for a new method of classification and treatment approach. Perhaps, in a process of negotiation that occurs over time, the primary care diagnosis of mental distress needs to consider the beliefs and attitudes of both patient and health care provider. Such a process may be overlooked by research studies that assess the patient at a single point in time, and could be the reason why many studies say physicians are slow to recognize the long-term emotional dimension to health care.

Health care providers can assess the willingness of the patient to discuss the sensitive topic of emotional distress by inquiring about stress and functioning in the patient's occupational and social roles. While some patients will indicate that emotional territory is off limits, patients who are willing to reveal their emotional distress can then be more fully assessed. Much of this back-and-forth is contingent upon on a stable and resilient patient-physician relationship.

Although health care providers should be comfortable with the diagnostic criteria for anxiety and depression used in psychiatric practice, many patients have discomfort that is not so easily labeled as all "body" or all "mind." But unfortunately, powerful disincentives, including a managed care environment that often forces patients to be split into "medical" and "psychiatric" components, as well as physicians and patients who are hesitant to confront mental disorders, tends to suppress the provision of necessary counseling and other treatments for emotional distress in primary care settings.

Another question is this: Given the constraints on their time and resources, are primary care physicians able to provide treatment for depression and other forms of emotional distress? Research suggests that patients with emotional distress would rather choose personal counseling over getting another prescription. But in the primary care space, significant obstacles of time and resources impede counseling, even when a physician's reluctance to investigate mental disorders has been overcome. Despite the barriers, some patients get counseling from their primary care physicians. Gallo recommended that health care providers become comfortable with at least one self-help manual, such as *How to Heal Depression*, or with the patient guide component of the guidelines. More than one publication discusses interventions that are both drug-free and appropriate for primary care settings.

While health care professionals sometimes downplay their importance in providing patient education, when information exchange takes place, patients express more satisfaction with medical care.

To improve how our health care system treats and supports patients whose illness has an emotional component, we need to develop new approaches to integrating mental health and primary health care. Accomplishing this goal will mean committing additional resources. Such an integration may also require mental health professionals to consider the primary care setting without their preconceived ideas gleaned from past experiences in specialty settings. For the evaluation and treatment of emotional distress, the primary care setting is key, and improving the therapeutic role of the generalist physician will lead to enhanced treatment for mental disorders in the community.

Research studies have linked clinical empathy to decreased physician burnout, better outcomes, greater patient satisfaction, and a lower risk of malpractice suits and errors. Systems are beginning to change. Beginning in 2015, the Medical College Admission Test added questions involving psychology and human behavior, recognizing that being a good doctor requires not just a grasp of science but an understanding of people. And in physician-compensation decisions, more than 70 percent of health networks and hospitals are now using patient satisfaction scores.

"The pressure is really on," says psychiatrist Helen Riess, director of the empathy and relational science program at Massachusetts General Hospital. Dr. Riess designed "Empathetics," a series of online courses for physicians. When it comes to promoting adherence to treatment and improving health outcomes, the accountability for health improvement serves to emphasize the importance of the unique relationship between patients and their doctors.

Empathetics teaches that empathic communication between clinicians and patients leads to a more engaged health care experience. With improved communication, patients who experience empathic care have better medical outcomes. In addition, adherence to treatment recommendations increases when medical professionals deliver patient-centered, compassionate care.

Empathy, patient engagement, and patient activation in and of themselves are positive, and reflect the growing recognition that our emotions play a central role in physical health outcomes, but they are limited in their reach. At the end of the day, unless we incorporate the stress level and subsequent compensatory behaviors into treatment, health outcomes will fall far short. People will feel more supported, but their health-interfering behaviors and overall health status will not have changed.

The basic standard of care should include an assessment of the patient's stress levels and the things that are causing that stress. The stress—compensatory behavior—disease state pathway should be on the wall of the office in the same way that the skeletomuscular system is on many provider's walls. Scores on these assessments should guide interventional strategies the same way that other lab values do.

Adjunct Providers in Emotional Dimension of Health

If a patient presents with little in the way of problematic compensatory behavior, then the primary care physician can suggest walks, naps, and herbal tea breaks. Should a patient's lab values be in a more problematic range and more health-interfering compensatory behavior is evident, a patient-centered approach would dictate a joint solution-orientated discussion to review the positive and negative consequences of the current coping mechanisms, as well as available alternatives. No one expects a physician to directly deliver physical therapy to her patient with a torn meniscus, nor should we expect the primary care physician to be able to directly build a patient's coping mechanisms, supports, and compensatory behaviors. In these situations, a physician working together with a stress coach could implement a plan using distress tolerance skill training, cognitive reframing, motivational interviewing, or emotional self-regulation skills.

Once these interventions have some positive effect, discussion can shift to new, health-promoting behaviors. For individuals whose needs are the greatest, medications and psychotherapeutic interventions might need to be an early-stage part of the treatment. As we've said over and over again—people are not going to give up the things that help them manage their lives day-to-day for some future state of physical well-being that is filled with anxiety. Adjunct health providers can offer these evidence-based tools for a kl wide range of patients.

Cognitive Reframing

If adverse childhood experiences can implant negative memories that support the body's drive to stick to an unhealthy baseline, following the process of allostasis described earlier in the book, then would it make sense to address those memories and shape them into something that is, if not positive, at least benign?

Many researchers think so.

First developed by Aaron T. Beck in the 1960s, cognitive reframing is a psychological technique that consists of identifying and then reshaping negative or destructive thoughts. It's a way of viewing and experiencing events, ideas, concepts, and emotions to identify more positive alternatives.

Beck worked with patients who had been diagnosed with depression, and found that negative thoughts, rooted in the past, would enter their minds. After encouraging his patients to recognize the impact of their negative thoughts, Beck helped them to shift their mindset to think more positively—eventually lessening or even getting rid of the patient's depression.

Now a core part of cognitive behavioral therapy (CBT), cognitive reframing recognizes that an adverse childhood event can be felt as either a major trauma or a challenge to be bravely overcome. It can see a stressful event as a learning experience, or depict a really bad day as a mild low point in an overall wonderful life.

Because once the ACE is long in the past, the body's current stress response is likely triggered by *perceived* stress, not an actual event.

Reframing techniques can change a person's physical responses to stress. If you perceive that you are threatened, either physically or psychologically, your fight-or-flight response will kick in. If you don't perceive a threat, your body will allow itself to relax.

One way to minimize the stressors you perceive in your life is to use reframing techniques, thus easing the process of relaxation. Here are three key steps that comprise cognitive reframing.

1. We Assign Meaning to Events

The first basic principle of reframing is that events or situations do not have inherent meaning; rather, people assign them a meaning based on how they interpret the event.

It can difficult to accept the idea that events or situations do not have meaning, but it's important if the patient wants to move ahead. Even when something seemingly horrible happens to them, it's only horrible because of the way they look at it. A good example is if you're walking through a field and you get struck by lightning. While the event was painful, clearly the event has no "meaning." You were just a random victim. Anyone else could have been struck by lightning. In the future, when you're going about your daily business at home and at work, you need not fear being hit by lightning.

This is not to trivialize tragedy. It's perfectly acceptable to be sad when something bad occurs. That being said, even a negative event can be given either no meaning or a good meaning.

2. You Frame Your Thoughts

The second principle is that behind every thought is a hidden "frame." The frame is a person's underlying assumptions and preconceptions that are implied by their thoughts.

For example, if Joe thinks, "I'll never get the promotion I want because I'm not the type of person who is unethical and must win at all costs," part of the frame is that only sharks get promoted. Since Joe believes that only sharks get promoted, as workplace events happen they will be interpreted within this frame. If someone else gets promoted, then Joe will conclude that the person must be an unethical and aggressive shark. Why would this impact Joe's health? Because Joe's stress levels will be unnecessarily heightened and he'll be chronically in his fight-or-flight mode. There is no bear chasing him, and yet he's running as fast as he can.

3. You're Trying to Ease Your Stress

The final principle is that behind every negative thought is a positive intention. When a person's inner voice expresses negativity, it's only doing so because it wants to help the person in some way. That doesn't make the thoughts always acceptable or right, but it does mean that the inner voice shouldn't be seen as an enemy to be defeated.

For example, when Dr. Felitti's obese patient said, "Overweight is overlooked, and that's the way I need to be," her inner voice—and her subsequent actions—were intended to provide relief from the emotional stress of having been raped the year before. Becoming physically unattractive to men may not have been the *best* response to her trauma, but it was a *rational and effective* response, and the one she was equipped to make.

By finding the positive intentions behind their thoughts, a person can work with their mind to find a positive reframe. That is far more effective than putting yourself down for having negative thoughts in the first place.

Cognitive reframing has been used successfully to treat addiction. "Addictive" thinking often includes rigid and self-centered perceptions that lead to resentments and great potential for relapse. In contrast, "recovery" thinking is expansive and empathetic, and directs the attention of the individual away from themselves and onto others. Recovery thinking leads to mindfulness and gratitude.

For example, an addict might say, "Ever since my parents learned I was using drugs, they've been trying to rule me and control my life. They hover over everything I do or try to do, and demand that I explain to them every place I go and whom I see."

Using reframing, a clinician's response might be, "It sounds like your parents care very much and, upon learning about your substance use, are struggling to learn how to best support you. This is a situation they've never encountered before, and their response may not be exactly what you want."

Regardless of the effectiveness of the parent's response, the therapist is trying to shift the patient's interpretation away something oppressive his parents are doing *to* him versus something his parents are striving to do *for* him.

As G. Alan Marlatt and William Henry George wrote in their 1984 article "Relapse Prevention: Introduction and Overview of the Model," published in *Addiction*:

"Both specific and global relapse prevention strategies can be placed in three main categories: skill training, cognitive reframing, and lifestyle intervention."

Skill-training strategies include both cognitive and behavioral responses to cope with high-risk situations. Cognitive reframing procedures can provide the patient with alternative thoughts concerning the nature of the habit-change process, and, for example, begin to view it as a learning process. Coping imagery can help a patient to deal with early warning signals and urges, and to reframe reactions to the initial lapse.

And then, while discussing gambling addiction:

"Why do some clients want to plan their own relapse? From a cost-benefit perspective, a relapse can be seen as a very rational choice or decision for many individuals."

With a gambling relapse, the emotional benefit can be immediate gratification and the chance of hitting the jackpot. For many gamblers, the promise of instant gratification far outweighs the cost of potential negative effects. Cognitive distortions such as rationalization and denial and make it much easier to approach one's own relapse episode by denying both the intent to relapse and the significance of long-range negative consequences.

When you rationalize, you're putting yourself in alignment with the way you think the universe operates. If gangs control your inner-city neighborhood, then joining a gang might be a rational choice. If you're depressed, eating cake might temporarily cheer you up. If you've been molested, becoming unattractive by becoming obese provides a place of safety and security.

Distress Tolerance

In the previous section I presented the scenario of a quiet walk in the woods that's interrupted by a bear. The bear chases you. Your fight-or-flight hormones surge, and you run. Then, when the bear has gone away, your body should return to its resting state so that you can continue your walk in peace. But it may instead remain in its fight-or-flight mode, and as a result you keep running, unable to stop. If your body remains at a level of high stress, then perhaps cognitive reframing might help you to distance yourself from the unpleasant shock and return to a comfortable condition.

But what if, when the bear approached, instead of going into full fight-or-flight mode, you could coolly run away? Think about running. The mere act of running does not elevate hormones or create stress. If it did, every recreational runner on earth would be emotionally pumped. In fact, most people fund running to be relaxing. Therefore, the act of running from danger doesn't create stress; it's the *emotional perception* of danger that is the stressor.

Here's another example. Chris and Taylor are sitting in a kitchen, drinking coffee. Suddenly a big spider crawls across the floor. Chris shrieks and jumps up on a chair. "Kill that nasty thing!" he or she cries (I'm being gender neutral here). In contrast, Taylor says, "Oh, look, a spider. Obviously I don't want to get bitten, so I'll be careful how I handle it. I'll just get a jar. I'll put the little fellow in the jar and toss him outside, where he belongs."

In both cases, the spider was a potential stressor, or source of distress. Chris had a low tolerance for this distress, while Taylor had a high tolerance. This matters because Chris's fight-or-flight hormones spiked, while Taylor probably felt nothing.

Distress tolerance is an emerging construct in psychology that, as Teresa M. Leyro, Michael J. Zvolensky, and Amit Bernstein wrote in "Distress Tolerance and Psychopathological Symptoms and Disorders: A Review of the Empirical Literature among Adults," published in 2010 in *Psychological Bulletin*, refers to an individual's "perceived capacity to withstand negative emotional and/or other aversive states (e.g. physical discomfort), and the behavioral act of withstanding distressing internal states elicited by some type of stressor." Other definitions of distress tolerance have also specified that enduring negative events needs to occur in contexts in which methods to escape exist—that is, seeing a spider on your kitchen floor is very different from being held up at gunpoint in a dark alley, where there is no escape.

In dialectical behavior therapy (DBT), the tendency of some people to experience negative emotions as unbearable and overwhelming is addressed with distress tolerance skills. Relatively low levels of stress can overwhelm people with a low tolerance for distress, and they may react with negative behaviors. Unlike many traditional treatment approaches, which focus on the patient avoiding potentially painful situations, the distress tolerance module of DBT teaches patients that on occasion pain will unavoidable and the best course is to learn to tolerate and accept some level of distress.

The concept of *radical acceptance* is a key ingredient of distress tolerance. This means that when the person is faced with something they cannot change, they choose to nonjudgmentally experience the situation and accept the reality of it. By practicing radical acceptance without responding emotionally or attempting to resist reality, the individual will be less vulnerable to prolonged and intense negative feelings.

Radical acceptance means being willing to experience a situation as it is now, rather than how you want it to be or imagine it to be. It means to be fully present in the actual situation you are in, rather than the situation you *think* you're in, or think you *should* be in.

As in the case of the spider, your mind is always going to give you other ideas and interpretations, and remind you of old strategies, whether helpful or unhelpful. Chris saw the spider as a fearsome enemy ready to strike and do harm. In contrast, Taylor saw the spider for what it was: a relatively small, nearsighted creature standing some distance away that probably had no interest in battling the gigantic humans looming over it.

Each time your mind wanders and you notice misleading thoughts and images, simply bring your attention back to the reality of the moment. Distress tolerance encourages you to not judge the situation to be either good or bad. Simply bring your attention back to the present moment, right now, this situation, and be effective in this situation. See not the fearsome adversary but the small arachnid who's equally afraid of you.

It does not mean judging every situation to be good. There are times when the spider could bite you, and there's no harm in recognizing this.

It does not mean giving permission for the situation to go on forever. It's okay to assert that the spider needs to leave the house.

It does not mean giving up your options. If killing the spider is what you have to do, then do it.

When used in the context of negative social determinants, such as when treating someone who lives in an impoverished, high-crime area, the concept of distress tolerance needs to be approached with great sensitivity. This is because it may be misinterpreted as encouraging people to accept substandard conditions rather than fighting to improve them. What should be kept in the forefront is that such approaches encourage people to see the reality of their environment and not let it produce destructive and unhelpful stress. This is not incompatible with wanting to improve your environment. To return to the spider metaphor, if necessary, you can choose to take action and kill the spider (that is, you can improve your environment). You can do this coolly and deliberately, without damaging yourself with a stress response.

Meditation, Mindfulness, and Healing

Meditation is a mind and body practice with a long history of use for coping with illness, increasing calmness and physical relaxation, improving psychological balance, and enhancing one's overall health and well-being.

Meditation comes in many forms, but most have four elements in common: a comfortable posture; a quiet location with few distractions; an open attitude of letting thoughts and distractions come and go naturally without judging them; and a focus of attention, such as an object, the sensations of the breath, or a specially chosen word or set of words.

While most people who practice meditation intuitively believe that it has a calming and rejuvenating effect, a number of research studies have investigated meditation's effect on specific disease conditions. These studies show that meditation may reduce blood pressure as well as symptoms of irritable bowel syndrome and flare-ups in people who have had ulcerative colitis. Symptoms of anxiety and depression, as well as insomnia, may also improve.

Research has indicated that meditation may physically change the brain and body, promote healthy behaviors, and help to improve a variety of health problems.

As the National Center for Complementary and Integrative Health (NCCIH) reported, a 2013 review of three research studies suggests meditation effects positive changes regarding aging. The practice may slow, stall, or even reverse changes that take place in the brain due to normal aging. And a 2012 NCCIH-funded study suggested that meditation can influence activity in the amygdala—which plays a major role in our emotions—and that different approaches to meditation may affect the amygdala differently, even when the person is not actively meditating. This suggests that meditation may lessen or reverse the long-term physical effects of adverse childhood events and negative social determinants, easing the body's state of perpetual stress.

As S. A. Gaylord and others wrote in their 2001 article "Mindfulness Training Reduces the Severity of Irritable Bowel Syndrome in Women: Results of a Randomized Controlled Trial," published in the *American Journal of Gastroenterology*, their research explored the "feasibility and efficacy of a group program of mindfulness training, a cognitive-behavioral technique, for women with irritable bowel syndrome (IBS)." The trial involved training the participants (the "mindfulness group") to intentionally attend to the reality of the moment while developing nonjudgmental awareness of emotions and body sensations.

Immediately after training and at three-month follow-up, women in the mindfulness group (MG) showed greater reductions in IBS symptom severity relative to the support group (SG). Immediately after treatment, changes in psychological distress, quality of life, and visceral anxiety were not significantly different between groups, but at the three-month follow-up researchers saw significantly greater improvements in the MG than in the SG. After treatment, mindfulness scores increased significantly more in the MG, confirming effective learning of mindfulness skills. When measured after the first group session, participants' ratings of the credibility of their assigned interventions were not different between groups.

Gaylord and co-authors concluded that the trial confirmed that mindfulness training reduced distress, improved health-related quality of life, and had a positive effect on bowel symptom severity. After group training, the beneficial effects lasted for at least three months—yet another illustration of the powerful link between emotions and health.

Motivational Interviewing

An evidence-based treatment that addresses a patient's resistance to change, motivational interviewing (MI) is a conversational approach in part developed by clinical psychologists Professor William R. Miller, PhD and Professor Stephen Rollnick, PhD. Growing out of their experience in the treatment of problem drinkers, the concept of motivational interviewing was first described by Miller in his 1983 article published in *Behavioural Psychotherapy.* In 1991, these fundamental concepts and approaches were more fully elaborated by Miller and Rollnick in a more extensive description of clinical procedures.

Essentially, motivational interviewing activates the hidden capability for beneficial change that everyone possesses. It's based in part on the idea that individuals with substance abuse disorders are *ambivalent* about their habit. Though they are usually aware of the dangers of their substance-using behavior, they continue to use substances anyway. They may feel the dichotomy of wanting to stop using substances while at the same time wanting to continue using.

Motivational interviewing seeks to facilitate and engage intrinsic motivation within the client in order to change behavior. It's designed to help people cultivate their interest in considering and/or making a change in their life, express in their own words their desire for change, plan for and begin the process of change, and strengthen their commitment to change.

Motivational interviewing is nonconfrontational, nonjudgmental, and nonadversarial. The approach attempts to increase the client's or patient's awareness of the consequences experienced, potential problems caused, and risks faced as a result of the behavior in question. Then, the therapist may encourage the client to envision a better future, and become more motivated to achieve it. "Change talk" can be elicited by asking the client questions, such as "How do you see this situation being different?" or "How does this situation interfere with goals you would like to reach?"

The clinician practices motivational interviewing with five general principles in mind:

1. Express empathy through reflective listening.
2. Develop discrepancy between clients' goals or values and their current behavior.
3. Avoid argument and direct confrontation.
4. Adjust to client resistance rather than opposing it directly.
5. Support self-efficacy and optimism.

Motivation for change is enhanced when the client perceives the discrepancy between their current situation and their hopes for the future. The clinician's task is to help focus the client's attention on how their current behavior differs from an ideal or desired behavior, and support them in their effort to change.

Care must be taken to let the client make his or her own discoveries. This is often called "the Columbo approach." As Miller wrote:

"Sometimes I use what I refer to as the Columbo approach to develop discrepancy with clients. In the old *Columbo* TV series, Peter Falk played a detective who had a sense of what had really occurred but used a somewhat bumbling, unassuming Socratic style of querying his prime suspect, strategically posing questions and making reflections to piece together a picture of what really happened. As the pieces began to fall into place, the object of Columbo's investigation would often reveal the real story."

Strategies for Patients

If you're reading this book and thinking about your own situation, there are things that you can do today to begin to move toward health.

First and foremost, give yourself credit for doing your best to manage negative feelings coming from your experience of trauma or toxic stress.

Second, acknowledge there may be healthier ways to cope and to build your strength going forward. As we've seen earlier in the book, compensatory behavior is intended to relieve emotional distress. From the perspectives of the emotional dimensions of health care and the vantage point of the patient, the "bad" habit is actually temporarily "good." This is because it serves a purpose in their lives to relieve distress. With this pivot in thinking on our part, our health interventions on people's behalf need to understand the compensatory nature of these behaviors. Change will not occur no matter how hard one tries if the needs being met by that behavior are not addressed through new behaviors or substitutes such as distress tolerance or other coping skills.

A partnership with a medical professional who understands the emotional dimensions of health care is invaluable. You may bring this book with you to your next doctor's appointment and talk with him or her about your interest in learning new compensatory behaviors that have the same stress management benefits with fewer deleterious health effects. If you do not feel comfortable talking with your current medical professional, it may be time to seek a new medical practitioner.

The following statements are examples of how you can help to start the conversation with your doctor:

- Some bad things happened to me as a child that I still struggle with.
- I'm very concerned about my children's safety.
- I do not sleep well on regular basis.
- I don't feel safe in my home.
- When I am feeling stressed or anxious, I find eating makes me feel better.

- I find that drinking alcohol helps me to relax and/or go to sleep.
- I am anxious about my blood pressure, heart disease, or diabetes.
- I rarely feel relaxed or comfortable. I have anxiety about the future.
- There are family issues in my past that I never talk about.

If you find it helpful, you can take the ACEs quiz online and bring the results to your medical visit.

If you're faced with a doctor who seems unwilling to listen and has a poor bedside manner, finding another health care provider doesn't have to be the only recourse. With narrowed insurance networks and waiting lists as the alternative, it might not even be the easiest. One potential solution is to speak up and ask your doctor to meet you halfway.

"What we recommend is that patients find appropriate ways to ask for what they need," psychiatrist Helen Riess told Elizabeth Renter of *USNews*. She suggests patients "lead with their vulnerabilities." Instead of thinking, "I didn't understand a word my doctor just said, and I'm not going back," Riess says a patient should speak out, and say, "I'm sorry, but can you put that into more everyday language for me?" Or, "You may not realize this, but I'm pretty anxious about this, and I need a few more minutes of your time to understand."

While your physician holds a degree from medical school and may bring years of experience to your treatment, that hardly means he or she is omniscient, and it's perfectly fine for you, the patient, to ask questions and want to know how the doctor can help you get better, not just today but tomorrow. In building good communications, you may have to take the lead—not just to have a better conversation but to help your physician guide you toward a lifetime of better health.

There are many self-caring actions you can take as well. Any form of physical activity that has been approved by your doctor is highly recommended. These can include things as simple as walking or the seven-minute workout. There are many new mobile apps such as Calm, Headspace, and MyStrength that have been demonstrated through research to bolster wellness.

Conclusion:

Making Emotional Dimensions of Health a Reality

My hope is that the preceding chapters have challenged, informed, and set in motion changes to your thinking about the emotional dimensions of the human experience and its incontrovertible impact on our health. A fair next question is, "How can we act on this knowledge in such a way to create real impact?" For reasons both historic and complex, our health care system today tends to look askance at our emotions. The introduction of the emotional dimensions of health care fundamentals presented in this book coupled with the illumination of practice pathways and targeting of research will take time and leaders to get to scale. After all, at its root, it requires a new direction to medicine in the US to move toward emotional dimensions of health and the reduction of chronic disease. Health care breakthroughs happen when there is overwhelming science, impact, and "buzz."

We have shown that in spite of extraordinary advances in medical technology and investments in health care, chronic diseases are getting the better of us. In America today our life expectancy is going down, more of us are sick, and we are paying far more than most countries for our health care.

We have also laid out the inextricable links between our emotions and poor health outcomes. While broader social policy and norms have much to do to reduce the negative effects of social determinants, medicine has the responsibility of assisting patients with the profound stress that these negative factors play in their lives.

Don Berwick, the physician who was the US Secretary of Health and Human Services and the head of the Institute for Health Care Improvement, once gave the commencement address at the Yale Medical School. In that address he said:

"All that matters is the person. The person. The individual. The patient. The poet. The lover. The adventurer. The frightened soul. The wondering mind. The learned mind. The husband. The wife. The daughter . . .

"Those that suffer need you to be something more than a doctor; they need you to be a healer. And to be a healer, you must do something even more difficult than putting your white coat on. You must take your white coat *off.* You must recover, embrace, and treasure the memory of your shared, frail humanity—of the dignity in each and every soul."

When you "join those you serve, you become a healer in a world of fear and fragmentation. That has never needed healing more."

The next generation of integrated care will be one that incorporates the critical role that *emotional distress* plays in our lives and in our health. From the most serious forms of trauma to our obsessive worrying, it all matters. And it all affects our health. We don't as yet have a health care system that is responsive to all of this, but I believe we can. The evidence is too clear—overwhelming in fact—and the outcomes too critical. We have the capacity to harness people's immense need to feel better, we have the means and technology to turn these too often health-interfering needs into health-promoting ones, and in doing so to understand how compensatory behaviors are linked to past and present personal experiences. We have the potential to put the power of our minds to influence our health care back with the body, but as we are doing so, understand how compensatory behaviors are linked to past personal experiences. By honoring the roles compensatory behaviors serve and by identifying new, healthy behaviors as replacements, we can improve people's lives, rekindle their faith in medicine, and ultimately achieve the Triple Aim for health care. There are a thousand journeys toward making the emotional dimensions of health a reality. I hope that you begin one today.

About The Author

David Woodlock's career as an innovator and leader in healthcare spans across the private, non-profit and government sectors.

He is currently President and CEO of ICL, an award-winning not-for-profit, human service agency offering health care, mental health care, family support, residential assistance, and treatment to nearly 10,000 adults, families, and children throughout New York City and Montgomery County, PA.

Previously, he was CEO at Four Winds Hospital, a private psychiatric system in upstate New York, where he was responsible for the overall executive leadership of the 88-bed inpatient services for children, adolescents and adults, an Adult Partial Hospital Program, and a Child and Adolescent Outpatient Program that serves over 5,000 individuals annually. During this time, he also led a major collaborative primary care and child psychiatry initiative.

Prior to his success at Four Winds, David Woodlock served in the New York State government for 32 years, including four years as a Deputy Commissioner of the NYS Office of Mental Health where he was responsible for the children and families system of care. During his tenure, he was successful in securing the largest annual appropriation for children's mental health services in the New

York State history; spearheaded an early intervention strategy that focused on schools and primary care; and, led the development of the first ever statewide Children's Plan. The Children's Plan represents a consensus of stakeholders throughout the system of care, 125 workgroup members and over 1000 participants in public forums, on best practices in comprehensive, coordinated social, emotional and developmental health for children.

Mr. Woodlock received both his Bachelor of Arts in Humanities and a Masters of Science in Special Education from Syracuse University. He was an Associate in Clinical Psychiatry at Columbia University's College of Physicians and Surgeons, as well as a Member of the American College of Healthcare Executives.

Mr. Woodlock has presented nationally and has written for several publications including Modern Healthcare regarding mental health systems and leadership, as well as programs for improving the mental health care of children and families. He has served on the Board of Trustees of the National Association of Psychiatric Health Systems and is currently Treasurer of the Coalition of Behavioral Health Agencies and Member of the Board of Directors of the New York State Coalition for Children's Mental Health Services.

He is the recipient of numerous awards, including the Extraordinary Leadership Award from New York State Coalition of Children's Mental Health Services; Special Congressional Recognition Award; and, the Social Justice Award from Syracuse University.